BRENT

Wembley, Willesden and Kingsbury

A Pictorial History

Borough of Brent's coat of arms, 1965. Prepared by the College of Arms, the design is based on that of its predecessor boroughs. For example, the lion is from the arms of Wembley and the dragon from Willesden. The Seaxes represent Middlesex and the wavy silver chevron represents the river Brent which once separated, and now unites, the two halves of Brent.

BRENT

Wembley, Willesden
and Kingsbury

A Pictorial History

Len Snow

Phillimore

1990

Published by
PHILLIMORE & CO. LTD.
Shopwyke Hall, Chichester, Sussex

ISBN 0 85033 752 6

Printed and bound in Great Britain by
BIDDLES LTD.
Guildford, Surrey

To all the young people in Brent
who are learning more about
their local heritage each week
and
to all those who were young in
Wembley, Willesden and Kingsbury

List of Illustrations

Frontispiece: Borough of Brent coat of arms

Acknowledgements

My greatest debt is to my wife Joan for her unfailing good advice and help, not least with the sheer task of typing the script, and also to others of my family, my daughter Susan, son Ralph and sister Rena, whose support and faith in the project has been marvellous. My next, and happy, debt is to Mr. Noel Osborne and Dr. John Stedman of Phillimore & Co., my publishers, for all their advice and encouragement. Grateful thanks are due to Mr. Geoff Hewlett of Wembley History Society and to Mr. Ivor Davies of Willesden History Society. Special thanks are due to Jack Blake, photographer-extraordinaire, and the many others who have helped in my research.

Finally I acknowledge my indebtedness to the Grange Museum and the various staff who have worked, or still work, there including Valerie, Irene, Tim, Bridget and Keith.

Despite all this help, such mistakes as may have occurred are solely my responsibility. Any notification of such errors will put the eagle-eyed observer in my debt, and in that of future readers.

Illustration Acknowledgements

The author wishes to thank the following for the use of illustrations: All Souls' College, 27; Brent Development Department, 2, 45, 49; Brent Housing Department, 46, 149, 150; British Geological Survey (Crown copyright reserved), 1; Dr. Richard Brock, 62; Terry Carton, 3, 5, 9; Desoutter's, 151; Grange Museum, 6, 10-12, 14, 16, 19, 22, 23a & b, 26, 30, 34, 36, 39-44, 47, 48, 51-56, 59, 63, 65, 66, 68-73, 75, 76, 78, 80, 81, 84-9, 93, 94, 96, 99-101, 106, 107, 110-13, 116-18, 120-24, 129-32, 135, 137, 140, 141, 144, 146, 154-56, 159-63, 165, 166, 168, 170-78; Greater London Records Office, 26, 28, 29; Guinness, 152, 153; Geoff Hewlett, 50; James James-Crook, 13, 32, 35, 74, 79, 82, 83, 102, 108-10; London Borough of Brent, frontispiece; London Borough of Camden, 33; London Transport, 104, 133, 134, 147, 148, 158; Des Mitchell, 119; Public Records Office, 8; St Robert Southwell School, 15; St Mary's church, Willesden, 20, 21; Wembley History Society, 24, 58, 59, 64, 67, 92, 115, 125-27. The following illustrations are the author's own: 7, 17, 18, 25, 38, 60, 61, 77, 90, 91, 95, 97, 98, 105, 128, 136, 138, 139, 141, 142, 145, 157, 164, 165, 167, 169.

Introduction

The district of 'Brent' is a political creation introduced in 1964 as part of a revision of local government in London. A quarter of a million people now recognise the former boroughs of Wembley and Willesden by their new name. Most people, however, think of themselves as living in a locality rather than in 'Brent', for example, Kingsbury, Harlesden, Alperton or Kenton. These names give us a clue to the history of Brent: they are not only districts within the present borough but are also the names of Anglo-Saxon settlements with a continuous history spanning over eleven hundred years.

The story begins even earlier. During the Iron Age, before London even existed, the Thames flowed through a large river basin, surrounded by hills and rocky outcrops. Small rivers flowed into the Thames, carving their own valleys between wooded hills. One such tributary was the river Brent. Iron Age nomadic tribes moved along the valleys of the Thames and its tributaries and then up the slopes of the hills to get away from the marshy river bed. They have left virtually no trace of their presence except the name they gave the river – Brent. This is a Celtic word, derived from the goddess Brigantia. Burial urns discovered in the 1880s during work on the Welsh Harp and flint axe heads found at Lower Place are almost the only material evidence of early man's settlement in Brent.

There is one striking piece of evidence of the presence of the Romans in Brent. This is Watling Street, now called Edgware Road or Kilburn High Road. Watling Street ran from Dover through London to Chester, and the stretch from Kilburn to Burnt Oak has been an identifiable eastern boundary for the district of Brent since Saxon times. By the eighth or ninth century Saxons were living in the area, as witnessed by local place names. Wembley was Wemba's leah or clearing; Harlesden was Herewulf's tun or farm; and Kenton was the farm of the tribe of Coena. In A.D. 767 King Offa granted land in Wembley to Archbishop Stidberht, while a charter of A.D. 825 refers to Wemba Leah. The pattern of Brent villages was probably established at this time and remained virtually unchanged for more than a thousand years.

The dominating influences on society in the Middle Ages were the Church and the King, who exercised his power through local chiefs like Herewulf, Coena or Wemba and, later, through lords of the manors. The strength of the Church derived not only from its physical presence in chapel or chantry at Harrow or Willesden but also from its landholdings. Canterbury owned part of Harrow parish, for example, St Paul's owned much of Willesden, while Westminster Abbey held land in Kingsbury. Early churches were mostly of wooden construction and so none have survived in Brent. Wembley was part of Harrow at this time so its religious centre was at St Mary's, Harrow-on-the-Hill. Willesden's church of St Mary was deep in the forests near the river Brent and is mentioned in a dubious charter of 939. The first building that can be physically identified dates from the 12th century, though only a few remains have survived. Willesden as a parish has existed for over a thousand years, the shape of the parish boundary virtually unaltered throughout all that time. Kingsbury's old church of St Andrew certainly has a few pre-Norman stones, but it dates mostly from the 12th century and later.

The local manors are listed in Domesday Book which gives a clear picture of the area in 1086. There were two manors in Kingsbury (one held by William the Chamberlain from the Abbot of St Peter's), one at Willesden and one at Harlesden (both held by the Canons of St Paul's), two in Twyford (also held by the Canons of St Paul's), and one at Harrow (held by Lanfranc, the Archbishop of Canterbury).

The Saxon system of local government, taken over by the Normans, was through the hundred, a district within the shire whose assembly of notables and village representatives, known as the moot, usually met once a month to adjudicate on local disputes. The moot for the area called Gore, which included Wembley and Kingsbury, met on a site near Kingsbury Circle – an inscription at the local police station records this historic link.

Rural Brent, 1086-1840

The layout of villages mentioned in Domesday Book in 1086 continued the basic pattern for many centuries. Willesden Green and Church End, Kilburn and Harlesden, Neasden, Kensal Green and Cricklewood, all part of the parish of Willesden, remained unchanged throughout. In that part of the parish of Harrow which became Wembley in 1846 were Wembley itself, Sudbury (at one time larger and more important than Wembley), Alperton (sometimes called Apperton or Appletown) and Kenton, Preston, Uxendon and Tokyngton. In the ancient parish of Kingsbury were Fryent and Roe Green, Tunworth and Chalkhill. Throughout the Middle Ages names of families with obvious local connections are common – Bartholomew de Willesden, Fulke de Brent, the Marshes and the Twyfords, to name but a few.

In 1086 the area supported a population of perhaps 500; by the time of the first national census in 1801 it had risen to between 1,600 and 1,700 – the exact figures are difficult to determine because Wembley was included with Harrow. This reflected a slow rate of growth, even allowing for the ravages of the Black Death in 1349. Kingsbury was particularly severely affected by the plague, so much so that the old village was largely abandoned and a new one grew up at the northern end of Church Lane around Kingsbury Green.

Many Wembley farms were sub-leased from the Church, other institutions such as All Souls' College, or large landowners like the Duke of Buckingham. Traditional methods of farming changed very slowly. Enclosures began in Harlesden and in parts of Wembley in the 16th century, but rapid change did not occur until the early 19th century. Wembley and Willesden were then the subjects of various Enclosure Acts and Awards between 1803 and 1823. Open fields disappeared, to be replaced by the familiar hedged fields, though these were later built upon because of demand for housing.

Long ago Willesden was divided into manors, reflecting its link with St Paul's Cathedral. Each manor supported a prebendary – the prebendal stalls can still be seen in the Cathedral. These manors were Willesden, Neasden, Oxgate, East Twyford, Harlesden, Chamberlayne Wood, Brondesbury and Mapesbury. Another was allocated to the Rectory and the tenth, West Twyford, was transferred to Ealing. Only one of the manor houses has survived: Oxgate Farm can still be seen on the eastern slope of Dollis Hill and is one of the two oldest secular buildings in the borough. Brondesbury Manor House was pulled down in 1934, having been home to a girls' boarding school in its final years. Neighbouring Mapesbury House had fallen victim to the incessant drive to provide more housing ten years earlier.

Neasden House was one of the grandest mansions in the area, standing prominently on top of a hill. It was the seat of the Roberts family, which played an important part in Willesden history in the 16th and 17th centuries. Sir William Roberts was a supporter of Cromwell during the Civil War and may even have approved the execution of Charles I. Various members of the Roberts family are commemorated by brasses in St Mary's church.

At one time the Archbishop of Canterbury had a local seat at Sudbury: the manor courts were held at Sudbury Court which later became a farm on the Northwick Estate. In 1957 it went the way of many other ancient buildings and was demolished during the construction of Kenelm Close. Originally, it was part of Harrow Manor which was subdivided to include Wembley Manor, Tokyngton (or Oakington) Manor, and also the Manors of Uxendon and Preston.

Uxendon Manor, a farmhouse, disappeared so long ago that there are no records of its physical appearance. It was, however, the scene of one of the most bizarre and exciting episodes in the history of the Brent area, the Babington Plot. This conspiracy of 1586 aimed to assassinate Queen Elizabeth I, release the imprisoned Mary Queen of Scots, and place her on the throne of England. Unfortunately, Babington revealed the entire plot to Mary and his letter to her, like all others, passed through the hands of Sir Francis Walsingham, Elizabeth's Secretary of State. Babington and four other conspirators were captured in August 1586 in a barn at Uxendon Manor, Harrow. Fourteen conspirators were executed at Tyburn in September and Mary herself was executed at Fotheringay Castle the following year.

Lyon Farm on Preston Hill was the home of John Lyon, one of the founders of Harrow School. After the house was rebuilt it became the home of the Perrin family who later gave their name to a small Council estate on the site of the demolished house. A small dwelling in Kingsbury known as Shell Cottage was part of Hyde Farm, built around the middle of the 18th century. Oliver Goldsmith stayed at the farm between 1771 and 1774 and wrote some of his best-known works there.

As a result of the religious changes during the Reformation, land in Harrow which had belonged to Canterbury Cathedral was given, in 1543, to Sir Edward North. This land later came into the possession of the Rushout family, one of whom became Lord Northwick. Part of Wembley had belonged to Kilburn Priory but during Henry VIII's reign passed to Richard Page whose family played a prominent part in Wembley's history. A later Richard Page created Wembley Park in 1793, employing Humphry Repton as landscape designer. It then passed to the Gray family who altered the White House mansion at Wembley Park (*see* plate 94). Tokyngton Manor came into the possession of the Read family during the Reformation. There was a chapel at the house, which could be used by local residents who would otherwise have had to walk to church at Harrow-on-the-Hill.

Willesden's church of St Mary had a national reputation for the holy shrine of Our Lady there, with its sacred black image which drew many pilgrims. Willesden's church lands, belonging to St Paul's, do not seem to have been affected by the Reformation and the Cathedral continued to act as an absentee landlord.

The two manors in Kingsbury referred to in Domesday Book were Tunworth and Chalkhill. Tunworth, dating from at least A.D. 957, was taken over by the Norman baron Arnulf de Hesdin at the time of the Conquest and was later granted to All Souls' College, along with other land in Kingsbury and land from the old manor of Malorees in Willesden. These gifts were made by Archbishop Chichele in the 15th century and provided a substantial source of income for the College. Chalkhill Manor originally belonged to Edward the Confessor, but passed to St Peter's (Westminster Cathedral) at the Conquest. Part then came into the possession of the Chalkhill family and another part, the Freyent Estate, was taken over by St Paul's in 1543.

Brent changed very little until the early 19th century. Willesden church is said to have been protected from the ravages of the 16th-century religious changes by Henry VIII's Vicar General, Thomas Cromwell, and one hundred years later another Cromwell, Oliver, may have protected St Mary's again during the Civil War because of his friendship with Sir William Roberts, lord of the manor of Neasden. The rural calm of this area was rarely shattered by national events. Crimes and disturbances did take place, and criminals were dealt with at the Courts Baron or, later, the Middlesex Sessions. The Napoleonic Wars brought hardship as the price of wheat was forced up, and Harrow had to raise its rates to pay for the increasing costs of maintaining the poor at the workhouse. The Agricultural Revolution brought improvements to farming methods. Wembley farmers turned more of their land over to pasture, Kingsbury and Willesden became hay-lands. A government investigation in about 1800 advised that much common land at Sudbury, Alperton and Wembley should be enclosed and this was duly done. The Industrial Revolution barely touched Brent at the start. The first sign of a changing world was the arrival of the canal.

Victorian Wembley and Willesden, 1840-75

Harrow-hill, standing, as it were, isolated and rising out of a rich vale to a very considerable eminence, affords a variety of beautiful prospects. The view to the East is terminated by the metropolis. (Lysons, 1795.)

At the entrance to the village, on the left, is Brandsbury House, the elegant seat of Sir Charles Coutts Trotter; nearly opposite, on the right, is an antique farmhouse. In a mile down the village, the Green is approached, which has been partly enclosed, but still retains the appearance of a sequestered spot. On the right on Dollar's Hill is Mr. Finch's farm, which, as an object from the valley below, has a pleasing effect. (*The Gentleman's Magazine*, 1822.)

These delightful pen portraits of rural bliss were soon to be pictures of the past. In 1801 a branch of the Grand Junction Canal (now the Grand Union) was cut through Alperton and Harlesden on its way to Paddington Basin and the Regent's Canal. The Brent Reservoir, or Welsh Harp as it is now known, was built to supply water to the canal, the feeder running south through Stonebridge. The system operated successfully for many years until traffic using the waterways was so reduced that it was no longer needed.

The arrival of the railways ended the short-lived success of the canals and encouraged the suburban expansion of London because they held out the promise of cheap and rapid travel. The world's first main-line railway was built by George Stephenson and opened in 1837 from Euston to Birmingham via Watford, bridging the Brent valley with a massive viaduct. The first local station was at Harlesden, though it was then called Willesden. This was followed in 1844 by another station at Sudbury, for Wembley. Soon a network of London railway lines began to cross Willesden, and Willesden Junction station was born. City workers could now move further away from the centre of London, especially as cheap workmen's fares were often offered. Together with the introduction of clean piped water (urgently needed after repeated cholera scares) and main drainage, this encouraged the outward expansion of London.

By a quirk of fate, Willesden, although half surrounded by London districts such as Hampstead and Paddington, was not swept into the Metropolitan Board of Works which later formed the basis of the London County Council. Nonetheless, it was along its south-eastern edge, closest to London, that urban development began in Willesden. Kilburn High Road itself was built up in a series of terraces, for example, Manor Terrace. Many large houses and farms which had previously lined the main road were demolished to make way for these terraces, the first of which was built in the 1850s, after the opening of the Kilburn station on the London to Birmingham line. At the entrance to Willesden, near the *Queen's Arms*, was Kilburn tollgate. It was removed from there, being repositioned further up the road several times. It was finally taken to the top of Shoot-up-Hill, but was demolished in 1872.

As one of the main roads out of London, Kilburn High Road (Watling Street) had a number of hostelries catering more for the traveller than the local resident. These included the *Bell* (on the Hampstead side) and the *Cock Inn*, both claiming to have existed since the middle of the 15th century. Kilburn Priory, just inside Hampstead, had offered respite for nuns in the 12th century and later provided hospitality to all travellers. On the same site, in the 18th century, were the highly-regarded Kilburn Wells.

Kilburn Park was designed, largely by James Bailey between 1859 and 1867, as a prosperous middle-class housing estate along Carlton Road (later Carlton Vale). Harlesden expanded, particularly when the busy Willesden Junction started to flourish, but it still remained the centre of a farming community. Kensal Green, stimulated by the opening of the famous cemetery in 1833, grew along the Harrow Road. Kensal Manor House was for many years the home of the famous Lancastrian novelist, Harrison Ainsworth, who lived in Kilburn before settling in Kensal. Many of his historical stories have links with Willesden.

In the mid-Victorian period Wembley and Kingsbury remained rural backwaters. Arable, cattle or pasture farming was the dominant activity. Farm workers from Ireland used to come each year for the harvest, sometimes sleeping rough in barns, as the 1831 census reveals. The first notable changes came through the influence of the Copland sisters, Anne and Frances, who promoted the building of St John's church in Wembley, or Sudbury as that part was still known. They also supported other philanthropic ventures including a school and a hospital. They built Sudbury Lodge as their home. The house later became Barham Mansion when it was acquired by Sir George Barham, founder of the Express Dairy, who established one of his model farms for dairy cows at Sudbury. This explains the name Farm Avenue. His son, George Titus Barham, became one of the great benefactors of Wembley between the wars. The mansion was demolished in 1956/7.

The different natures of rural Harlesden and urban Kilburn led, in the 1870s, to a vitriolic debate within the Willesden parish. Kilburn residents wanted legislative power to set up an elected Sanitary Authority; Harlesden residents felt that they would be paying for Kilburn's sewers! Eventually, in 1875, government approval was obtained and the first local government election took place in Willesden. Among those elected was George Furness, a builder who had been the main contractor for the Thames Embankment and had campaigned against local government powers. Also elected was F. A. Wood, a notable antiquarian and one of the leaders in the fight for 'independence', that is the right for Willesden to control its own affairs as an elected Board.

Expansion, 1875-1900

Between 1888 and 1898 Willesden was the fastest growing district in Greater London. From the nucleus in Kilburn Park, virtually the entire 'peninsula' south of Queen's Park station was quickly built up. Kilburn High Road became a continuous stretch of shops with flats above and the urban development extended to Cricklewood, Kensal Green, Harlesden, Willesden Green and Stonebridge. At one time, four houses were being built in the area every day. Property developers, the largest being the United Land Company, bought up farms such as Bramley's (sold by Catherine Nicoll in 1877) and large mansions such as Gowan House, both near Willesden Green. They then developed estates of small villas on roads connected only to the High Road, not to adjacent streets.

In a similar fashion the fields of Stonebridge disappeared, becoming 'Poets' Corner', though large houses nearby survived, including that owned by F. A. Wood, the historian of Willesden. Cricklewood was partly developed by George Furness, while at Kensal Rise the ever pressing demand for more housing thwarted the plan for a National Athletics Ground. The open area between Queen's Park and Salusbury Road became yet another housing estate, while further north All Souls' College allowed development on its land. So rapidly were houses built in Willesden that Gus Elen could sing:

> By climbing up the chimbley
> You can see acrorss to Wembley
> If it wasn't for the 'ouses in between!

Some of the new housing estates commemorate their links with historic owners through the names of roads: Dean Road and Chapter Road are a reminder of St Paul's Cathedral; Anson Road and its side streets such as Heber, Oman and Dicey all recall All Souls' College, Oxford. Incidentally, the Church Commissioners, known then as the Ecclesiastical Commissioners, forbade the building of any more public houses on their land in Willesden.

Wembley developed around the station, though at a slower pace. Elsewhere, however, links with the past remained: large houses like Wembley House, the White House (Wembley Park) and Barham Mansion, and, at the other end of the scale, farm cottages such as those which are still standing in Sudbury Court Road or Elms Lane.

The expanding community did not neglect its children. St Mary's School had existed near the church at Willesden since the 1820s and in 1849 the Copland sisters set up the first 'public' school, Sudbury National, at St John's church. After the 1870 Education Act Harrow local council opened schools at Sudbury and Alperton. The Church of England opened others in south Willesden and the Roman Catholics soon followed suit. Whitehall stepped in to stop this piecemeal development of educational facilities and insisted that Willesden should establish a Local Education Board to expand schools to meet rapidly developing needs. Within a few years several elementary schools had been built in Kilburn. Small and short-lived private schools sprang up in Kilburn, Kenton, Kingsbury and elsewhere. In the 1880s, for example, there were about a dozen such small schools in and around Willesden Lane alone.

The rapid growth of the area encouraged the Church of England to divide its existing parishes. As a result, Christchurch was created at Brondesbury in 1866, Holy Trinity at Kilburn in 1867, St John's at South Kilburn in 1871, All Souls at Harlesden in 1879, and St Augustine's in 1880. The last named was the magnificent masterpiece of J. L. Pearson, its spire dominating Paddington, on the boundary of the area under consideration in this book. Other denominations also built to meet the needs of their congregations. There was a Congregational chapel at the junction of Willesden High Road and Dudden Hill Lane from about 1820 to around 1903. This accounts for the name Chapel End, which complements the original Church End half a mile down the road. Roman Catholics were able to resume the public celebration of their faith after the church of Our Lady of Willesden was built in 1907, a reminder of the medieval shrine. This church was rebuilt in 1931.

Horse-drawn buses were providing a regular service from Harrow to London in 1825 and for many years afterwards. In fact, a stage coach had run from Harrow to Holborn as early as 1681. Local railway stations such as Wembley were served by buses ferrying passengers from neighbouring villages. By the end of the century there were regular and frequent horse-drawn bus services from Kilburn and Harlesden to various destinations in central London, operated by the London General Omnibus Company. The first horse-drawn tramway in north-west London was opened in 1888 and ran from Amberley Road, Paddington, along the Harrow Road to Harlesden Green; the fare for the entire journey was just twopence!

In 1863 the first underground railway was opened between Paddington and Farringdon Street via Baker Street. In 1879 a branch line was opened which crossed into Willesden at Kilburn and stopped at Willesden Green before ending its run, for the time being, at Harrow-on-the-Hill. The Metropolitan line was the brainchild of a remarkable man – Sir Edward Watkin. He dreamed of a railway from Manchester through London and then a Channel tunnel to Paris. Sadly, many of his schemes came to naught. These included a construction which he hoped would rival the Eiffel Tower. It was started in Wembley Park, opened as an amusement park in 1894, but never rose above the first floor as the money ran out. It became known as Watkin's Folly before it was demolished in 1907. It was on this site that Wembley Stadium was built in 1922-3. More of a success for Watkin was Neasden Village, including Quainton Street which was built to house railway workers from the nearby depot. The nearest 'industry' at that time was Jackman's smithy in Neasden Lane.

Late Victorian and Edwardian Brent, 1895-1914

In 1895 Wembley and Willesden both became Urban District Councils with considerable powers of local government, though these were shared with the relatively new (1888) Middlesex County Council. Wembley included the parish of Kingsbury but it was an ill-matched marriage and, in 1900, Kingsbury became an Urban District Council in its own right. Willesden planned and built a town hall in Dyne Road to reflect its elevated status. It was a handsome Victorian building but was demolished in the 1970s to make way for council flats. Wembley's civic buildings were in the High Road at the junction with St John's Road, now the site of a large store.

An anonymous verse composed in 1894 claimed that

> Weary man may sleep serene
> In lovely sylvan Willesden Green.

This was a romantic view even in 1894, and ten years later the area was not 'sylvan' at all. The relentless growth of suburban London before the Great War engulfed almost the whole of Willesden south of the Metropolitan railway line – an official, but very temporary, boundary. Wembley was also developing slowly around the station known from 1882 as Sudbury and Wembley, and also up on Wembley Hill. Meanwhile, the recreation centre called Wembley Park (on the site of the earlier estate of the same name laid out by Humphry Repton, centred on the White House) was converted into a successful amusement park with a lake, golf course, tea pavilions and, for a while, Watkin's Folly. The park closed during the Great War.

The early councils paid much attention to the prosaic but essential subject of sewage disposal. First Willesden (as a Sanitary Authority in 1875), then Wembley, and finally Kingsbury, all sought sites for effluent outfall, often provoking opposition from neighbours. There were frequent complaints from Wembley, for example, about the smell from Willesden's sewage farm at Stonebridge. O. C. Robson, Willesden's first Board Surveyor, and Dr. C. E. Goddard, Wembley first Medical Officer of Health, both made a great contribution to the improvement of the local environment. The new Urban District Councils were also responsible for roads, street lighting, the fire service, by-law applications, and education.

Councils were given greater responsibility for education in 1902. While Middlesex County Council retained overall control of schools, Willesden was one of a number of 'Part III' authorities given oversight of elementary schools, the new secondary schools being allotted to the county. The continuing growth of Brent needed to be matched by a corresponding increase in the number of schools and churches. These came in quick succession: schools in Leopold Road, Stonebridge, Mora, Oldfield and Park Lane; St Andrew's, St Michael's and All Saints, St Gabriel's, St Matthew's, St Anne's and St James's churches.

As the pace of building quickened, it became more and more important to retain open spaces. The new councils reluctantly made themselves responsible for this and it is to them we owe Roundwood Park, Gladstone Park and King Edward's Park. Queen's Park was a gift to the City of London from the Church Commissioners, making use of the site of an earlier Royal Agricultural Show.

'The Poor' were cared for largely by the Boards of Guardians. Willesden had its own Board after 1896 and in 1903 opened its Workhouse/Infirmary on the Twyford Abbey Estate at Lower Place. Eventually it became the Central Middlesex Hospital. Prior to the existence of this workhouse, the Willesden poor were sent to Hendon Union's workhouse at Redhill, Edgware.

In the 1890s W. B. Luke pursued a well-organised campaign to secure free public libraries for the area, starting with Willesden. In quick succession libraries were opened in Willesden Green, Kilburn and Harlesden, followed soon after by a reading room at Kensal Rise which was opened by the American humorist, Mark Twain. Wembley's needs were at first served through the County Council, but no branch library was opened until 1952, at Barham Park.

Street and domestic lighting by gas was introduced to Willesden in the 1870s, under the direction of O. C. Robson, but Wembley had to wait until 1894. Soon this source of energy was overtaken by electric power. Willesden Council built an electricity station at Taylor's Lane, sold it to the Northmet Electric Company and then acted as municipal supplier to the Borough until nationalisation in 1948. Telephone services were initially provided by private companies until these were taken over by the Post Office. The first telephone exchange in the area opened in Harlesden in 1896.

Before the Great War, firms like Comben and Wakeling had begun to build houses along St John's Road and then the Stanley Park Estate, near the Wembley Triangle. Other builders began developing the Curtis Estate to the west of Ealing Road and the Wembley House Estate which became London Road and its neighbouring streets.

Kingsbury remained largely rural except for some development along the Edgware Road. Many large houses such as Lewgars, Kingsbury House and Chalkhill House survived, as did many farms.

The network of railways which criss-crosses Brent was almost completed with the building firstly of the Great Central extension (part of Watkin's dream of the Manchester-Paris route) through Sudbury and Wembley Hill, later Wembley Stadium station, and then the District extension, an electrified line which ran through Ealing to Alperton and on to Uxbridge and later became the Piccadilly line. Electrification was then introduced on the Metropolitan line and allowed for the development of the next ring of suburbia which included 'Metroland' in Wembley, Pinner and beyond. Another enterprising use of electricity gave the tramway network a great boost, despite the surprising opposition of the L.C.C., which prevented its extension along Kilburn High Road. Most of the other main roads in Wembley and Willesden were soon provided with economic electric trams.

Before the start of the Great War Willesden was home to a considerable number of industrial firms. One of the oldest was the signal engineering firm of Saxby and Farmer at Kilburn. McVitie's opened their biscuit factory at Waxlow Road, Stonebridge, in 1906. There were small engineering firms in Lonsdale Road, Queen's Park, and a wide variety of manufacturing companies large and small in other parts of the borough. Wembley was less developed industrially, but early firms included a motor works in Lancelot Road, Wooller's 'Flying Banana' motor cycles in Alperton (the site was taken over by Glacier Metal in 1923), and the British Oxygen Company in north Wembley.

Homes for Heroes, 1914-1940

During the Great War many engineering firms in Brent converted to the manufacture of munitions. Kingsbury became a minor aviation centre with airfields at Stag Lane, Grove Park and Kingsbury Green. A housing estate was specially built at Roe Green for the aircraft workers, though it was only partly completed by the time the war ended. The site of the Park Royal Exhibition offered land for factories – the forerunner of the huge industrial estate which developed after the war. The war took a terrible toll of local men, mainly soldiers, and war memorials were erected in churches, schools and public places, respectfully recording the great sacrifice made by citizens of Brent.

When the war ended the Prime Minister, Lloyd George, declared that he wanted 'to make this a fit country for heroes to live in'. Willesden was one of the first authorities to respond to the government's plea for more houses. The estate at Stonebridge was the first, although, unfortunately, it had the newly-built North Circular Road as its western boundary. Wembley soon followed with the Christchurch Estate off Ealing Road, while Kingsbury reluctantly built Highmeadow Crescent. These efforts, the start of a drive for council housing, were soon matched by the march of private developers over the green fields of Wembley and Cricklewood. Suburbia was born and a love-hate relationship with London soon emerged. 'Metroland', the name coined by the estates subsidiary of the Metropolitan railway, was largely responsible for this enterprise. Its foresight in buying land on either side of the extension to Harrow and beyond enabled developers to provide a series of housing estates and gave John Betjeman the subjects for some of his finest poems.

Other developments which totally changed the appearance of much of Brent north of the Metropolitan line were undertaken by firms such as Laing, which went on to build a national reputation, Comben and Wakeling, and also Costin, more locally based. Some had a recognisable style, like Comben and Wakeling's 'Tudorbethan' half-timbered

Sudbury Court Estate. Callow and Wright built the Neeld Estate in Tokyngton. In 1933 prices for such houses ranged from £685 to £975 for a typical three-bedroomed house, with or without garage. A special mention must be made of the architect, E. G. Trobridge, whose thatched houses and four 'follies' enliven Wakeman's Hill in Kingsbury.

In the 1920s Wembley succeeded Willesden as one of the fastest growing London districts, while in the 1930s Kingsbury emulated them both. Green field after green field disappeared to be replaced by housing estates complete with shops, a school, places of worship, public houses, and a small open space to remind residents of the countryside that had been lost, as in Tokyngton or Sudbury Court. An attempt was made by Wembley Council to secure Wembley Park for housing but the British Empire Exhibition proposals overtook it.

As new housing spread over the north of Brent, slum clearance took place in Kilburn. In 1934 Alpha Place was demolished and residents were rehoused in the newly-built Curzon Crescent Estate, the name providing another link with All Souls' College. It was not only the slums that were razed to the ground. The big houses continued to fall victim to the rampant developer. Neasden House (which became Neasden Golf House, then flats as Neasden Court before ultimate demolition), Brondesbury Manor, Mapesbury Manor and Wembley House were all lost at this time.

The inter-war housing developments were matched by the spread of industry, aided by improvements in the transport system. To the network of railways used for freight, some through private sidings, was added the new North Circular Road which, in Willesden, was specially built as part of the ring arterial road. Regrettably, 'ribbon building' was not prohibited until 1935. However, the new road did open up Staples Corner, while Western Avenue, just outside Brent, helped to make the Park Royal industrial area accessible to traffic. On Dollis Hill the Post Office Research Station (1934) made a striking new addition to the Neasden skyline. During the Second World War its basement was occasionally used for cabinet meetings. Guinness built its superbly-designed factory at Park Royal in 1934, initially encouraging the misleading story that it had been built for the conversion of potatoes to motor spirit! Many industrial estates sprang up, often taking over the sites of wartime factories as in Kingsbury and Park Royal. The General Strike of 1926, which brought ten days of bitter struggle, had its effect on Brent. Willesden Council, while not Labour-controlled, broadly supported the strike, although it insisted on maintaining electricity supplies. In Wembley, voluntary support for the strikers divided those who helped from those who 'had a go' at driving buses to town.

Willesden Cottage Hospital, later Willesden General, had been a late Victorian gift from the Cornish philanthropist, Passmore Edwards. Wembley Hospital opened in 1928, supported by local benefactor G. T. Barham. Willesden had its own municipal hospital in Brentfield Road, originally for those with infectious diseases. It later became Neasden Hospital and, as part of the N.H.S., was converted into a geriatric hospital and then sold off and demolished.

With the invention of film, the cinema swiftly became a prominent part of the High Street scene. Europe's largest cinema, the Gaumont State in Kilburn, opened in 1937. Over 30 cinemas opened in the area during the 40 years from 1910, but then, within another 20 years, completely disappeared from Brent until the State was re-opened as a smaller cinema in the 1980s. Wembley almost became the British Hollywood as film companies established themselves on the former Empire Exhibition grounds. Sadly, fire and loss of confidence led to the scheme's collapse. Some isolated film making also took place at various sites in Willesden from 1918 onwards and, more recently, television companies have opened offices and studios in the district.

Borough status was a prize coveted by many District Councils. In 1934 Willesden and in 1937 Wembley (reunited with Kingsbury) both achieved this ambition. Sadly the Mayor-designate of Wembley, George Titus Barham, who had contributed so much to his town, died on the day the charter was sealed.

Post-War Brent, 1940-75

The Second World War had a much greater impact on the home front than the First. Nearly 2,000 homes in the area were destroyed and 24,000 were badly damaged. People lived under constant threat of death from bombs, mines, V1s and V2s but the expectation of ultimate victory led to talks on post-war reconstruction at both national and local level. Willesden optimistically prepared plans which included the almost total redevelopment of South Kilburn. Nonetheless, initial efforts had to concentrate on rebuilding or repairing homes and other buildings which were the material casualties of the war. Wembley was able to concentrate more on new council estates at Sudbury Farm, Fryent and Kingsbury.

'System-building' became the catch-phrase of the day and tower blocks began to dominate the local horizon. Massive new housing estates were created in the 1960s and 1970s to replace older houses at Stonebridge, Chalkhill, Church End and South Kilburn. In the 1980s private developments began to gather momentum as government restrictions on council building were enforced.

Industry at Brent, having boomed between the wars, found the post-war period more difficult. Factory after factory in Willesden closed. Some were converted into smaller industrial units, some became warehouses, some were rebuilt as residential housing estates. At the same time, however, there was an expansion of office development, particularly along the North Circular Road and at Wembley Park.

In 1964 local government was again re-organised. Wembley and Willesden boroughs were yoked together by the London Government Act of 1963, which also created the Greater London Council. The name chosen for the new borough was that of the river which had previously separated them, Brent, and the motto 'Forward Together' well expressed the hope that unity would prevail. This was perhaps an unrealistic hope as Wembley had been Conservative dominated since its formation and Willesden had been wholly Labour. The arguments which flew across the council chamber at Wembley (Willesden town hall was pulled down to make way for council flats) were reminiscent of those between Wembley and Kingsbury councillors in 1899. In 1965 Brent started to deal with problems handed over by its predecessor authorities. Housing, education, social services, refuse collection, road maintenance and parks all became the responsibility of 66 councillors and thousands of dedicated staff. (Until 1974 there were 60 councillors and 12 aldermen.) The citizens of Brent form part of the multi-ethnic and multi-cultural fabric of modern society. Movement into the area from overseas, not to mention those who have come from Wales, Scotland and from other parts of England, has been taking place peacefully for nearly 200 years. Irish labourers, Jewish refugees from Russia and later from Nazi Germany, Caribbean and Asian families have all settled in Wembley, Willesden and now Brent. The new borough has the distinction of being the most multi-racial district in the country. Some schools have children from 30 or more countries, speaking as many different languages.

Royal Brent

The royal family is no stranger to Brent. Over the last hundred years, every British monarch has visited Wembley, Willesden or Brent. One local school even bears the name of a member of the German royal family – Princess Frederica C of E Primary School in Kensal Rise.

An early royal visitor was Queen Victoria who attended the International Exhibition of the Royal Agricultural Society in July 1879. This was held on some one hundred acres of land between the stations now called Kensal Rise and Queen's Park, the latter specially built for the occasion. Despite heavy rain, the show was a great success. Part of the site is now Queen's Park recreation ground. Victoria's Golden Jubilee in 1887 was celebrated in Willesden with a whole range of festive activities, and the Jubilee Clock at Harlesden is a permanent testimonial to the affection felt for that monarch. At Anson Road there used to a clock commemorating the coronation of George V but it was removed for road widening. In 1901 the Royal Agricultural Society returned to Willesden looking for a permanent site for its annual shows. It leased a large plot in the west of the district near the stations on the Great Western and the new District (later Piccadilly) lines. In 1903 the area was named Park Royal in honour of the Prince of Wales, later George V. Unfortunately, bad weather again spoilt the opening of the show and, as it was no better in the following two years, the Society abandoned the site. Munitions factories were built there during the Great War and in 1934 Guinness acquired part of the site for its brewery.

Before the Great War ideas for an Empire Exhibition had been mooted, but it was not until 1921 that a scheme began to take shape. Royal patronage helped make possible the erection of Wembley Stadium on the site of Watkin's Folly. King George V opened the British Empire Exhibition on 23 April 1924 and it was generally regarded as the greatest exhibition ever held in London. Because of its success, it opened again in the summer of 1925 and 27,000,000 people visited it during these two years. The displays represented either the cultures and crafts of the member countries of the British Empire or the spirit of enterprise of the mother country. The displays were housed in large pavilions such as the Palaces of Industry and of Art which still survive, and in many smaller units. The 'Never-stop railway' carried visitors round the vast Exhibition and was itself one of many marvels which attracted the multitudes. After the Exhibition, one of the kiosk holders, Arthur Elvin, purchased the site, including the Stadium, and converted it into a successful entertainment complex which is still operating today. Another part of the site was developed by the adjoining railway company as a factory trading estate and this, too, is still flourishing.

In 1948 Britain was host to the Olympic Games and Wembley Stadium was the venue for many of the events. The Marathon race finished in the streets of Wembley before the final turn into the Stadium itself. During the 1908 Olympics, the shooting events were held at the Uxendon Shooting Club and a halt was built next to the Metropolitan line at Preston Road. Members of the royal family have attended Cup Finals and many other important events at the 'Home of Football'. Wembley has expanded its sporting activities to include speedway, greyhound racing and, with the building of the Empire Pool, swimming and later ice skating.

* * * * *

The illustrations which follow expand on this outline history. For convenience, the name Brent has been used in all the captions when referring to the entire area even though, strictly speaking, it can only apply after 1965. The illustrations reproduced in this book represent only a small proportion of those which exist, and readers may be interested to look at others held at the Grange Museum of Community History in Neasden Lane.

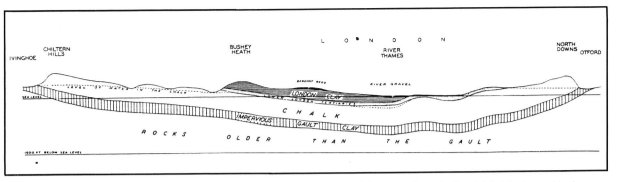

1. The effects of the Ice Age were felt almost to the edge of London and, in retreating, glaciers left behind gravel beds, boulders and other evidence. The Thames valley, then wide and marshy, contained a number of tributaries such as the Brent which flowed sluggishly between wooded hills.

2. The River Brent was formed by the two head-streams of Dollis Brook and Silk Stream which joined in the middle of what is now the Welsh Harp (Brent Reservoir). The river receives three tributaries – the Wealdstone, Slade (or Mitchell) and Wembley Brooks. The river system created hills such as Wakemans, the highest in Brent at 302 feet, Dollis and Wembley and Mount Pleasant.

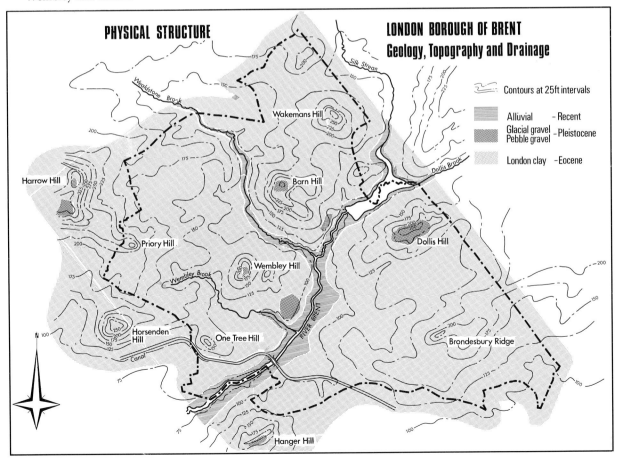

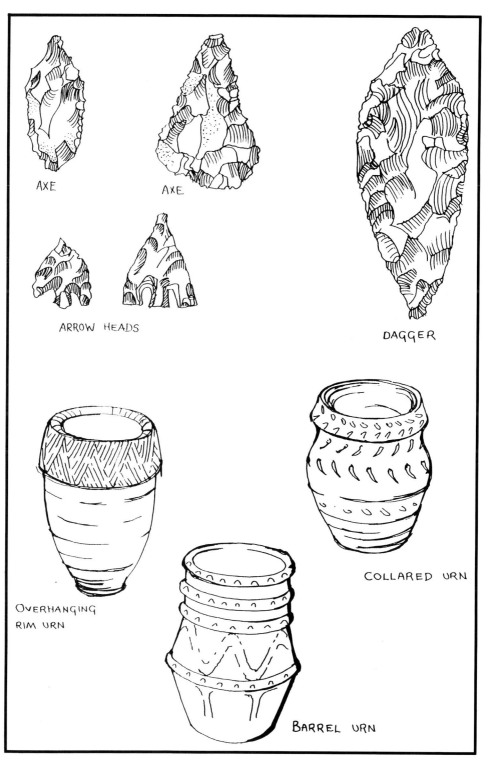

AXE

AXE

ARROW HEADS

DAGGER

OVERHANGING
RIM URN

COLLARED URN

BARREL URN

3. Celtic and British tribes left behind little evidence in Brent of their physical presence. There have been a few finds of flint axes, bronze axes (at Lower Place, Disraeli Road), burial urns (beneath the Welsh Harp) and relics of the Iron Age, but these have been so sparse as to suggest the absence of settlers along the upper Brent valley. There were, however, some Stone and Iron Age settlements on Horsendon Hill to the west of Brent.

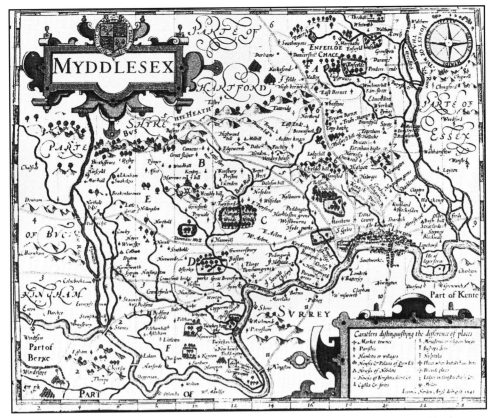

4. The earliest map of London appears to date from 1560, but the first with a wide distribution was John Norden's print of 1593. Although small, it shows the City of London within the county of Middlesex and the Brent villages dating from Saxon times – Wilsedon, Nesedon, Wembly Hill, Preston, Kylbourn and Kingsbury.

5. St Mary's, Willesden, as it may have looked in the 15th century. The earliest part of this church dates from the 12th century, but it is likely that it was preceded by a wooden Saxon building. The earliest known rector was 'John, son of German'. In the Middle Ages churches were the focus of village life, even though in Willesden this meant a walk along a winding road through woods and fields, and in Wembley a trudge up the hill to St Mary's, Harrow-on-the-Hill.

6. St Andrew's, Kingsbury, is thought to be one of the oldest churches in Middlesex. A building almost certainly existed in Saxon times, but the present structure, although incorporating some older material, dates from the 12th century with, as is the case in St Mary's, later additions.

7. Hundreds were divisions of the shires in this part of Anglo-Saxon England, Willesden coming under Ossulstone Hundred. The Gore Hundred Moot met in a triangular-shaped field ('gore') at Kingsbury. This inscription is cut into the wall at Kingsbury police station which stands on the site of the Moot.

MIDELSEXE.

WELLESDONE tenent canonici S pauli. p xv. hid' se defendebat sep. Tra. e. xv. car. Ibi uilli. viii. car. 7 vii poss fieri. Ibi. xxv. uilli. 7 v. bord. Silua qngent' porc. In totis ualentiis ualet vi lib. 7 vi. sol. 7 vi. den. qdo recep. similit. T.R.E. xii. lib. hoc ñ tenen uilli ad firmá canonica. In dnio nil habet. h maner' fuit de dnico uictu. T.R.E.

HANDONE. ten' abb S petri. p. xx. hid se defend. Tra xvi. car. Ad dñ111 pan'. x hide. 7 ibi fuit 111 car. Uilli hnt. viii. car. 7 v adhuc poss fieri. Ibi pbr ht. 1. uirg. 7 111 uilli qsq. dim' h. 7 vii uilt qsq. 1. uirg. 7 xvi. uilli. qsq; dim uirg. 7 xii bord qtenes dim' hid. 7 vi. cot' 7 1. feru. ptu. 11. boii. Silua mille porc. 7 x. sol. In totis ualent' uat viii. lib. X do recep. similit. T.R.E. xii lib. hoc ñ iacuit 7 iacet in dnio eccle S petri.

8. Domesday Book, compiled at the direction of William the Conqueror in 1086, sets down the land-holdings 'as they were in 1066 and as they had become in 1086', to paraphrase the document. William had taken land from the Saxons and presented it to his Norman barons; one of the two Kingsbury manors was handed over in this way.

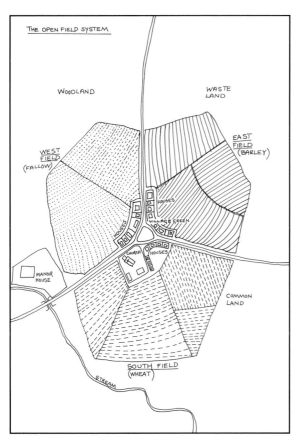

THE OPEN FIELD SYSTEM

WOODLAND

WASTE LAND

WEST FIELD (FALLOW)

EAST FIELD (BARLEY)

HOUSES

HOUSES

VILLAGE GREEN

HOUSES

CHURCH

HOUSES

MANOR HOUSE

COMMON LAND

SOUTH FIELD (WHEAT)

STREAM

9. In the Middle Ages the church was the spiritual centre of the town and the manor, with the squire, was the secular focus. Sir William Roberts of Neasden held such a position in the 17th century, although the system did not always operate in Brent according to this model. The land was cultivated in strips allocated to individuals, with a three-yearly crop rotation. Common land including the green was just that – held in common by the village.

10. The Willesden inclosure map of 1823. The change from the open-field system to enclosed fields, which gave the countryside the patchwork effect seen today, took place in Brent, as elsewhere, unevenly over a 250-year period. Between 1803 and 1823 most of the remainder of Brent was enclosed under separate awards for Willesden and for 'Harrow otherwise Sudbury', which included Wembley. This map for Willesden shows the field boundaries, greens and roads.

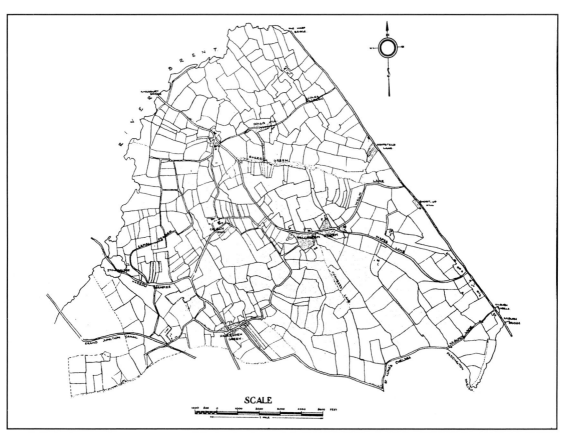

SCALE

11. Oxgate Farm in the 1950s. With 100 Elms Farm this is one of the two oldest secular buildings in Brent. It was the centre of Oxgate Manor, although not its manor house. Bartholomew de Willesden (see Plate 20) farmed here, and William of Wykeham, founder of Winchester College and of New College in Oxford, was a prebendary. During the Great War its meadows were secretly used by the Tank Corps, which explains the naming of Tankridge Close.

12. Twyford Abbey was built as a private mansion in 1820 but, ironically, in recent years it has been used as a nursing home by the Alexian Brothers, a religious order. It was the grandiose scheme of Thomas Willan who bought the West Twyford farmhouse and had it rebuilt as a 'cockney-Gothic' battlemented mansion by the architect W. Atkinson who later built Abbotsford for Sir Walter Scott. This photograph was taken in 1900.

13. The manor was the focus of many villages, but was not as obviously dominant in either Wembley or Willesden as in other country districts. The ten manor areas in Willesden are clearly identified as most of them had a manor house, often a glorified farmhouse. Brondesbury Manor is one such example, the photograph depicting a 19th-century replacement in its last phase as a girls' boarding school, c.1910.

14. Mapesbury Manor, c.1860. A manor house probably existed on this site from the late 12th century. It was named after Walter Map, one of the first prebendaries of the manor. By the 15th century, parts of this and other Willesden manors had been given over to form a manor for Peter de Malorees, and it later formed part of All Souls' College's large landholding in this area. This 19th-century building was pulled down in 1925 and replaced by Coverdale and Deerhurst Roads.

15. Saint Robert Southwell. The story of the bizarre and tragic happenings of the Babington Plot which was centred on Uxendon Manor is worthy to have been told by Harrison Ainsworth. The owners, the Bellamies, gave aid to Catholic priests such as Robert Southwell who were fleeing from Elizabeth's agents, and also to Anthony Babington who was implicated in the plot to assassinate Queen Elizabeth and replace her with Mary Queen of Scots. Southwell, who wrote a number of fine poems while imprisoned, was later canonised and a school in Kingsbury is named in his honour.

16. Sudbury Court, *c.*1935. Sudbury was once the local seat of the Archbishop of Canterbury who, before the Dissolution of the Monasteries, owned much of Harrow. This 17th-century farmhouse was entitled to the name Sudbury Court. It later came into the ownership of the Perrin family, by whom it was sold for demolition in 1957, Kenelm Close being built on the site.

17. 100 Elms Farm. This two-storey red-brick building was erected in the 16th century, probably as part of a larger farm, perhaps that of the Archbishop of Canterbury's Sudbury demesne. The building lies within the former dairy depot and is therefore difficult to photograph.

18. The Grange Museum. Now the home of Brent's Local History Museum which opened in 1977, the Grange was originally part of the outbuildings of The Grove, which was built in about 1700 by Thomas Wingfield and pulled down in the 1930s. The Grange had early been converted into a house by James Hall and continued as such until its present use.

19.   Neasden House in the 1920s. The big house on top of Neasden Hill existed in some form from the 14th century. It was the seat of the Roberts family, but after their decline in the late 17th century it changed hands several times. In the 1920s it became Neasden golf house, then flats and was finally demolished. All that remains of the group of fine houses round Neasden Green is the Grange Museum itself.

20. Brasses in Willesden church. Monuments in churches can tell us a great deal about local history – as can a study of tombstone inscriptions in the churchyard. There are many brasses in St Mary's, including this one dating from 1492 of Bartholomew de Willesden, who leased Oxgate Farm, and his wife.

21. This 1585 brass of Edmund Roberts shows him with his two wives and their nine children. He was the great-grandfather of Sir William Roberts, parliamentarian and squire of Neasden.

22. St Mary's, the parish church of Willesden, was probably extant in A.D. 938 and is seen here in a rather idealised engraving of 1750. This south view shows it in a truly rural setting, with Neasden Hill in the background to the left.

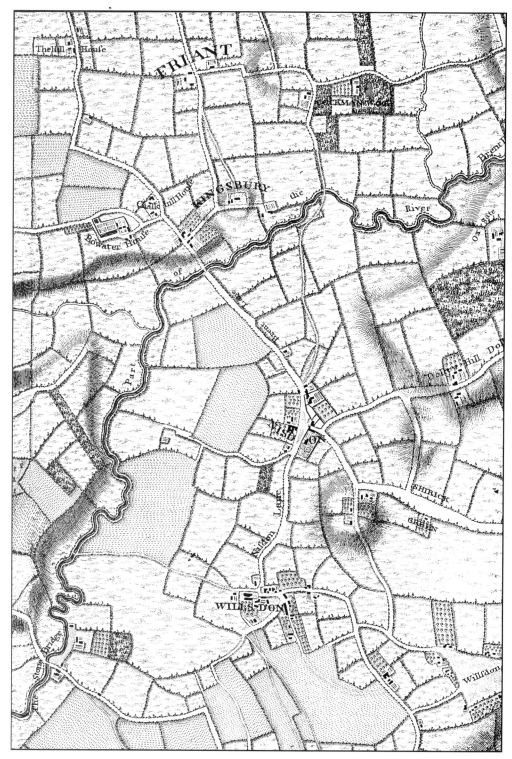

23 a. & b. The Willesden and Wembley sections of John Rocque's map. The first maps of London appeared in the middle of the 16th century. One of the earliest to extend beyond the metropolis was John Rocque's map of 1745, its considerable detail of hedgerows and trees contrasting with the starker line drawings on Warburton's map (see plate 26). Wembley Green, on the hill, is the nucleus of the later town, and this map would have been little changed if it had accompanied Domesday Book.

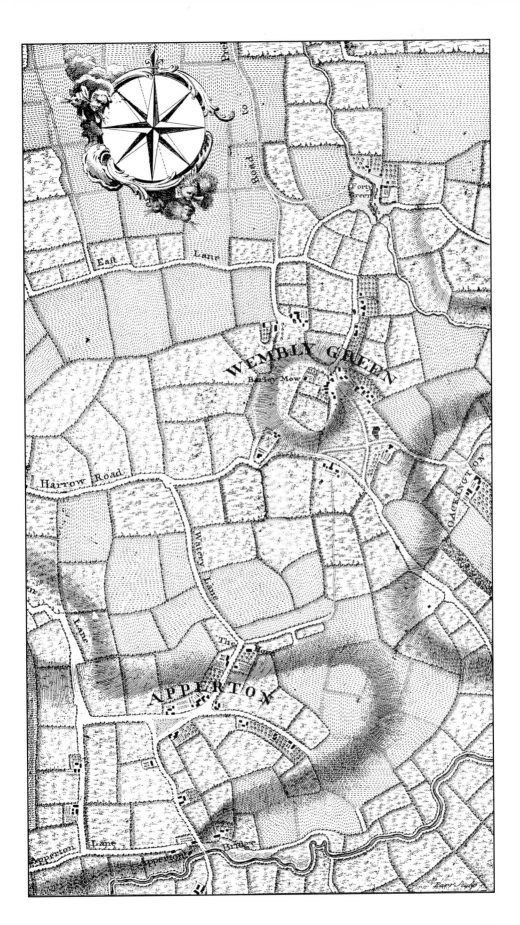

24. Lyon Farm in 1939. This early 18th-century farmhouse is the successor to that owned by John Lyon himself. He was one of the founders of Harrow School, which was only two miles away in the same parish. The farm was later taken over by the Perrin family who left it to Wembley Council in the 1960s, when it was demolished and replaced by a small, pleasant housing estate called John Perrin Place.

25. Shell Cottage, Kingsbury. Hyde Farm (the name is derived from the term 'hide') was one of a number of farms in this agricultural community. Its special distinction is that its owner, Edward Selby, loaned a room to the writer Oliver Goldsmith between 1771 and 1774 where he wrote works such as *She Stoops to Conquer* and was visited by Boswell. Shell Cottage, in the grounds of Hyde Farm, is now the only link with the old estate.

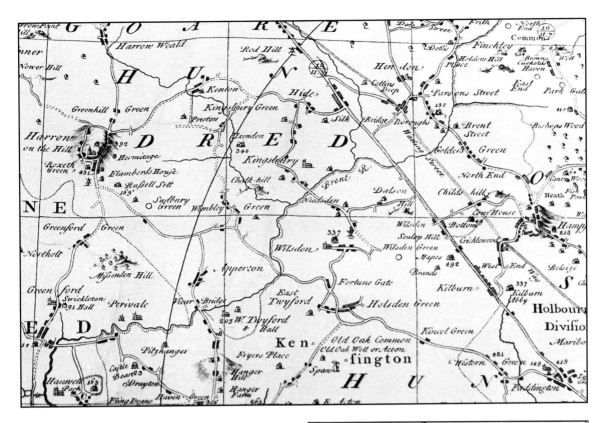

26. Warburton's map, 1749.

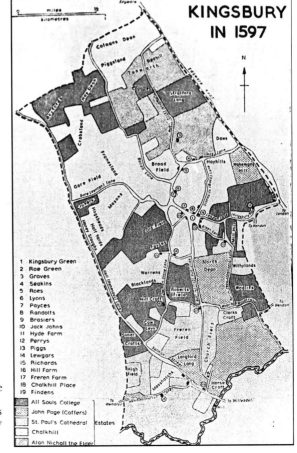

27. Kingsbury's land holdings changed slowly over the 500 years after the Norman Conquest as did the rest of Brent. This map of 1597 shows not only the large holdings of All Souls' College and St Paul's (relics of the Domesday manors) but also the many farms, greens and common fields.

28. Greenwood's map of 1819, which can be compared to that produced by Warburton (see plate 26). This map is one of the earliest to adopt the current spelling of Willesden.

October y 27: 1725

It is this Day ordered & agreed upon at a Vestrey by us whose names are here unto Subscribed that the sum of one penny in the pound Is Granted towards the Repairs of y Highways

Henry Amoss senior
Daniel Hawkins
Samuell Greenhill
Henry Hinch
John Robinson
William Newman
Tho Thompson
John Bond
Benjamin Lawrence
Thomas Vincent
Joshua Wade
Francis Hawkins
James Grant
Joseph Coker

29. Harrow vestry records, 1725. From an early date civil and criminal matters were dealt with either through parish vestry meetings or by the courts baron or leet, which came under the manor. These could appoint local officials such as the beadle, constable, ale-conner and hayward, and from the 16th century they had rating powers. These hand-written minutes, dated 27 October 1725, fix the highway rate at one penny in the pound.

30. *The Old Six Bells* in Church End near St Mary's, *c.*1860, one of the few old inns to have disappeared. It was the favourite haunt of the Willesden vestry as it was near the church, which is hidden by the trees to the left. The letterbox on the wall was used from 1870 for letters to London, collected every morning at nine and every afternoon at four. The new magistrates court has been built on this site.

31. The Welsh Harp at the end of the 19th century. This dam replaced the structure of 1835 which burst with tragic results in January 1841. Before this date it had, sadly, claimed the lives of four Sidebottom brothers of Roe Green who were bathing in the reservoir in 1835 as it was being completed.

32. 'The Jolliest Place That's Out' was a song referring to the *Old Welsh Harp*, the long-established inn from which the reservoir drew its name. From 1859-89 it was run by W. P. Warner who made it a place of resort for the whole of London with water-sports, a concert hall, a museum of animals and fish, and even its own station on the Midland Railway. It was needlessly destroyed to make way for the North Circular Road flyover.

33. The London and Birmingham Railway, 1835. The first trunk railway was opened as the London to Birmingham in 1837 from Euston via Watford. The first station was at Harrow, Harlesden (then named Willesden) following in 1842 and Sudbury (for Wembley) in 1844. The crossing of the Brent valley at Stonebridge was a major engineering feat which involved moving 372,000 cubic feet of earth from Oxhey to build the embankment. The original bridge, with a main arch of 60 feet and three land arches on either side, survives. This picture shows the bridge at Kenton Road before the station was constructed.

34. Harlesden Manor House, the farm at the heart of rural Harlesden, *c.*1860. The opening of Willesden Junction station in 1866 hastened the urban development of this area and heralded the demise of the village.

35. The bridge carrying the Hampstead Joint Railway (later the North London Railway) over the Edgware Road at Brondesbury station pictured some time between 1860, when the line was opened, and 1879 when the Metropolitan Railway crossed the road further up. Shoot-Up-Hill can clearly be seen in the distance.

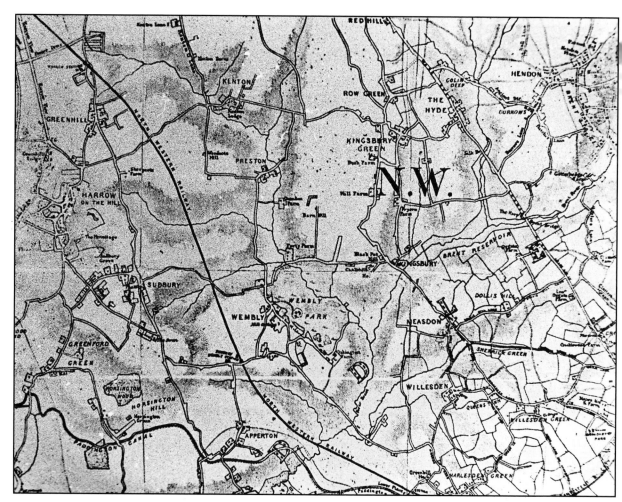

36.   This mid-Victorian map of north-west London was produced by Stanford's, the well-known map-makers, and shows clearly how rural Brent still was in 1864. Many familiar names can be seen, including Wembly (*sic*) Park, Oxgate Farm, Oakington Farm, The Hyde and Queens Town, and only two railway lines are in evidence.

37. The earliest development in Kilburn was along the High Road and the area towards Carlton Vale. This block of shops with flats above was built in the 1870s and in the centre, beneath the chimneys, the name 'Manor Terrace' is carved in stone, now somewhat worn by time and weather. The style of the stone window openings varies on each level, producing an exciting architectural texture.

38. These houses in Cavendish Road, built in the 1860s, were part of the early development of Brondesbury when the North London Railway came through from the City, and the ecclesiastical commissioners who owned the land found they had a goldmine. Although a few of them are still 'Pooter-style' family houses, they are much in demand as flats.

39.   This photograph of Kilburn tollgate was taken in about 1860 before it was moved further up Kilburn High Road. *The Queen's Arms* (a few yards outside the borough) is behind the photographer to the left, and Goubert's nursery is on the right on the site of what became the Kilburn Empire.

40.   The River Brent forms a considerable barrier to movement and until recently there were only four road crossings on each of the main roads in and out of London. Pictured here is the Brent Bridge (*c.*1799) on the Edgeware (*sic*) Road, showing the river before it was dammed to form the reservoir. On the far side is the *Old Welsh Harp* (see plate 32).

41.   An 18th-century print of *The Bell Inn* on the Hampstead side of the Edgware Road (now Kilburn High Road) with Kilburn tollgate in the distance. The size of the forecourt of the inn indicates how far forward the modern hostelry has moved. From the inn sign hung not only the sign of the bell but also two sheaves of hops.

42.   Although Mill Lane is on the Hampstead side of Shoot-Up-Hill, the famous Old Mill on the summit was on the Willesden side at the corner with Mapesbury Road. It burnt down in 1863, a few years after this photograph was taken, and was replaced by a steam-driven mill.

43. Cock Inn Gardens. This extract from an old *Willesden Chronicle* tells the story of the row of cottages behind the *Cock Inn* at the corner of Victoria Road and Kilburn High Road. It was common practice for the gardens behind inns to provide space for cottages, as at the *Spotted Dog* in Willesden Green. The cottages mentioned here were demolished in 1925.

44. Although Kilburn Priory (1722) was in Hampstead, it had many connections with Willesden. Originally a hermitage, it became a nunnery and acquired land in Kilburn, Wembley and elsewhere. It was often visited by travellers, particularly pilgrims en route to St Albans or Willesden. After the Dissolution (1545), the priory came into secular hands and the buildings had disappeared by 1814.

THE PASSSING OF "COCK GARDENS."

' Tuesday's sitting of the Willesden trict Council, mention was made of impending closing and demolition of ny of the cottages in Victoria Place, and the Cock Tavern, High-road, Kil n. Mr. Howard Barnard sends us the owing account of this old piece of inal Kilburn :—

The two charming sketches which I e may accompany the

aval. Very little is known about the inn until about exactly 500 years later, 1762, when the ' Cock,' the pond adjoin ing, and the old pound tall of which are indicated on Rocque's map of 1745), were devised by the late proprietor, William Lamplough, of Wokingham, to a certain Jeremiah Crutchley, of Clarges-street, Piccadilly. In 1800, the said Jeremiah sold ' the Cock inn and messuage adjoin ing ' to two people of the name of Jen nings, and in 1813 the property was in the possession of John Walmsley,' inn-

are roofed with pantiles, and built of re dish stock bricks of a kind similar those used in the making of the 500 yea old stables in Dudden Hill Lane recent pulled down; the garden wall at Doll Hill House, and other old buildings st standing in different parts of the paris Builders are of opinion that bricks we made locally in the 18th and early 19 centuries: and readers of this journ may remember that in my articles, d ring the war period, on ' Willesden Stre Names,' I pointed out that Victoria-ro

45. Houses in Cambridge Avenue. The impact of the railways on suburban London was crucial. Yet in Kilburn the opening of the station in the High Road in 1851 initiated a very slow pace of development. The main road received the first expansion but it was ten years before the Kilburn Park Estate was begun. James Bailey was the builder and the quality of his buildings, many of which are now listed, has ensured their survival.

46. Houses in Princess Road, dating from 1859-67, which have been successfully restored.

47. *The Old Crown*, Harlesden, *c*.1860. Harlesden village expanded round its green but in the 1860s, before Willesden Junction station opened, it was still part of a small rural community. *The Royal Oak* stood at the other, eastern, end of the green near the so-called Manor House. The man on the left in a white apron may be Mr. Clary, the publican.

48. Sellons Farm, c.1896, one of the large farms in Harlesden. The brothers John and William Sellon were commissioners for the Willesden Enclosure Award. Eventually the farm fell to the advance of bricks and mortar, and all that remains is the name Sellons Avenue, where building started before the end of the 19th century.

49. No. 175 High Street, built in 1847, was part of the expansion of Harlesden village, anticipating the 'new' Willesden Junction station due to open a few months later. Its simple elegance is protected by local listing and by sympathetic refurbishment by a housing association.

50. Cottages in Harrow Road, Kensal, which are among the loveliest in Brent. They were built from 1816-24 along the Harrow Road opposite the yet-to-be-built Kensal Green Cemetery. Some of the larger houses in the same stretch of the road are equally full of charm and character.

51. This 1750 sketch of the *Old Plough* at Kensal Green is an 18th-century view of a 16th-century building, one of the haunts of the painter George Morland.

52. Kensal Lodge in the Harrow Road where Harrison Ainsworth, the novelist, lived for a short period. His main home was next door at Kensal Manor House which has been demolished, and the site is used by a scaffolding firm. This photograph was probably taken in the 1930s (note the trolley-bus wires) but the building dates from about 1820 or a little earlier.

53. In the mid-Victorian period this was still a very rural area as this view of Dollis Hill Lane near Dollis Hill House shows. The photograph was taken in the 1870s, years before the land on the right became Gladstone Park. The lady standing by the carriage is a Miss Metcalfe from Richmond Villa in Cricklewood.

54. Sudbury Priory, like Twyford Abbey, was built for private use and not as a religious house. It became a school in the 1930s, but was empty by 1939 and, although in good condition, it was used as a training ground by the Home Guard during the Second World War. The priory was later demolished and replaced by the houses of Priory Gardens.

55. Wembley Green's leading inn, *The Green Man*, seen here in the 1860s, went through a variety of names – a practice long established and still continuing, as a study of the public houses on Kilburn High Road would reveal. On the Rocque map (see plate 23) it is shown as *The Barley Mow*. Its position on top of Wembley Hill ensured that it was much visited for its views of the surrounding district.

56. Kingsbury was the last area of Brent to be developed and this was the village-inn appearance of *The Plough* at Kingsbury Green until the mid-1930s, when it was rebuilt. This photograph was taken *c.*1906.

57. *The Red Lion, c.*1890. This photograph of The Hyde section of the Edgware Road reveals the state of the main roads at that time when there were persistent complaints of poorly-maintained highways in Kingsbury.

58. Soon after Sudbury Hall was built it was taken over by the Shaftesbury Society as a home for destitute girls. Here they were trained for domestic service, the matron for many years being the redoubtable Miss Chipchase. In 1930 the Society moved and the building was converted first into flats and then into a police barracks. In the 1970s it was demolished to make way for a new police station.

59. Cottages at Sudbury, c.1890, built by Sir William Perkin (1838-1907) who achieved renown as the discoverer of aniline purple dye, and who came to live in Sudbury, eventually at The Chestnuts. He built a workman's hall in the village near *The Swan* and these cottages behind.

60. Villages in Wembley, Willesden and Kingsbury changed little in the 800 years after the Norman Conquest. These cottages, No. 116 Elms Lane, on the Sudbury Court Farm, have survived since the late 18th or early 19th century.

61. Several small cottages, such as Nos. 96 and 98 Sudbury Court Road pictured here, have managed to survive in parts of Brent despite threats from housing developments. The protection and refurbishment of these 18th-century houses was made possible by an agreement that two further houses could be built next door in a matching style in the late 1980s.

62. Anne Copland, c.1850. John Copland acquired Crab's House in 1801 and, on his death, the estate passed to his daughters Frances and Anne. They used their legacy for the benefit of their home town, building St John's church, a school, a hospital and their own Sudbury Lodge, later called Barham Mansion. Anne died in 1872, two years after her sister.

63. A charming view of Crab's House, later called Old Barham Court, *c.*1920. Following the deaths firstly of the Copland sisters and then of George Titus Barham, the estate was bequeathed to the local council and this building is now used as a library and for other community purposes.

64. The Copland sisters provided the first 'public' school in Wembley, a National School under the auspices of the National Society run by the Church of England, next to St John's church. After 30 years it was supplanted by Alperton School in Ealing Road which was run by the Harrow Board of Education. This building, pictured in 1920, burnt down in 1971.

65. St John's church, Wembley, c.1920. The Copland sisters were responsible for the building of this church in 1846 on the low ground near the Wembley Brook, rather than on Wembley Hill as some residents had proposed. Sir John Gilbert Scott, the architect, later designed St Pancras station, the Albert Memorial and other buildings in the Gothic Revival style.

66. One of the saddest losses to the borough was Barham Mansion. Built by the Copland sisters in the 1850s, it took its name from the family who founded the Express Dairy. With the onset of war, the building deteriorated despite having been bequeathed to Wembley Council whose duty it was to maintain it. By 1957 the cost of rehabilitation was considered too high and, by one vote, the Council agreed on demolition. This photograph was taken in 1920; the balustrade in the foreground is all that remains today.

67. This photograph of the Harrow Road near Barham Park and a tram bound for Sudbury, with the Old Court on the left, was apparently taken in winter, possibly during the First World War. Chaplin Road was later built on the extreme right.

68. Welford's Dairy, Harlesden, 1923. Following the success of Barham's Express Dairy, others were established to supply London with milk. This dairy was later taken over by United Dairies, now Unigate.

69. Vale Farm Dairy, Sudbury, *c.*1910. Although the giants of the dairy world like Express and United Dairies came to dominate the milk supply industry, small firms such as this (and later Dowling's Dairy in Wembley) offered direct farm-to-home delivery. Milk was ladled, none too hygienically, from the big churn into small cans for the individual household.

70. The son of the founder of Express Dairies, George Titus Barham (1859-1937), took over the family firm which had settled in Wembley in 1880. G. T. Barham, seen here *c.*1920, became involved in his adopted town as a benefactor, councillor and charter mayor. He suffered from a deformity of the spine, but his strong spirit carried him through a successful life. Tragically, he died the day the Charter was granted.

71. In the inner London area, a form of Metropolitan fire brigade had succeeded the insurance companies' private, often conflicting, brigades, but in the mid-Victorian suburbs, for protection against fires, people still relied on volunteers. Here in Willesden in 1874, the local volunteer fire brigade have some basic equipment to which they would need to harness a horse commandeered from the nearest street.

72. Another group of volunteers, the Victoria Rifles, *c.*1854. They gave their name to Victoria Road, Kilburn. The entrance to the rifle ground, on the right, is next to Holy Trinity School, and off to the left is a smithy and *The Cock Inn.*

73. Local services such as drainage, roads and street lighting were paid for by local rates, which were the long-established means of raising money, but the vestries had limited powers. This official notice about the poll in Willesden's Board in 1873 concerns the adoption of the Local Government Act in Willesden; in 1875 Willesden Board was created. New legislation set up democratically-elected sanitary authorities.

74.   The lodge of Roundwood House. George Furness (see plate 75), one of the founders of modern Willesden, was a successful civil engineer. He built himself a beautiful mansion, Roundwood House, in Longstone Avenue, named after the Derbyshire village where he was born. This is the road leading to the lodge in the 1890s; the house itself can be seen in plate 76. Harlesden Road, on which the lodge stood, has been considerably straightened, and today Knowles House would be on the right.

The late **Mr. G. Furness,**
Chairman W.L.B.
1875—1881.

Mr. F. A. Wood,
Chairman W.L.B.
1881—1888.

Mr. J. Stewart,
Chairman W.L.B. & W.D.C.
1888—1896.

Mr. H. T. Reed,
Chairman W.D.C.
1896—1897

Past Chairmen of the
Willesden

Local Board & District
Council.

Mr. W. Ginger,
Chairman W.D.C.
1897—1898

Mr. C. Pinkham, J.P., C.C.
Chairman W.D.C.
1898—1900.

75. George Furness can be seen in this rare 1875 picture of the Willesden Local Board. This included F. A. Wood the historian and James Stewart who built the town hall in Dyne Road, which has now been replaced by the flats named in his memory. Although Furness fought against the introduction of local government, he embraced it when the vote went against him and became first chairman of the Local Board. Furness Road is named after him.

76. This sumptuous Gothic mansion (*c.*1880) was Roundwood House, the home of George Furness in Roundwood Park. Sadly, it fell victim to demolition contractors.

77. A remarkable survival amidst the large-scale redevelopment of Stonebridge, 'Hurworth' was built in about 1890 by F. A. Wood, the Willesden historian and one of the co-founders of local government in the district (see plate 75). His many volumes of meticulously written historical notes form the basis of every history of Willesden. His former home is now the Stonebridge Park Conservative and Unionist Club.

78. Saxby and Farmer's, Kilburn, c.1880. One of Willesden's earliest industries, this railway signals engineering works was founded in the 1870s in Canterbury Road. It survived for many years but eventually most of the industrial buildings were demolished.

79. A view of a busy Kilburn High Road in 1898 from Kilburn Bridge. A horse-bus on its way to town is overtaking two hansom cabs. The Willesden side of the road is to the left and the bank on the right still stands on the corner of Belsize Road, although under a different name. Indeed, most of the buildings in this scene remain unchanged.

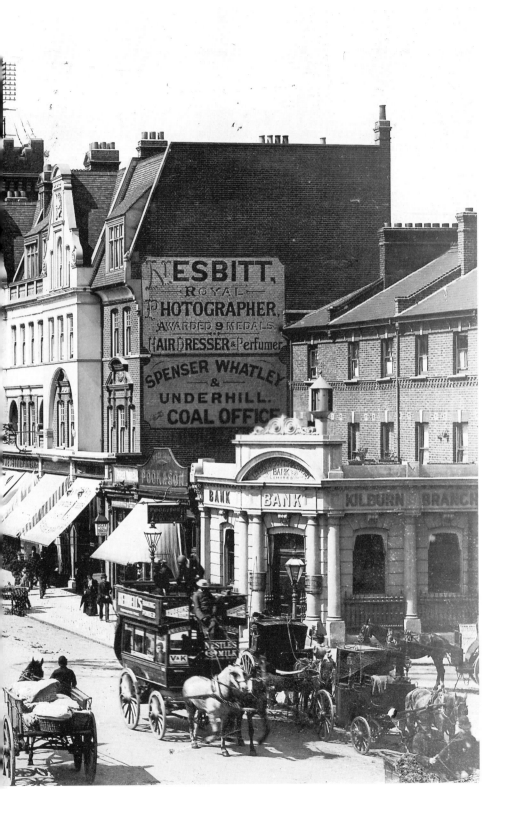

80. Bramley's Farm, Willesden Green, *c.*1870. Two neighbouring farms between Willesden Green and Dollis Hill (seen in the distance in this photograph) were acquired by the United Land Company for building. The Metropolitan Railway burst through in 1879 and created opportunities leading to the disappearance of rural Willesden. The shape of the roads and estates reflects the piecemeal unplanned development of the area. Bramley's vanished under Villiers and Chaplin Roads.

81. Hodgson's Farm, Willesden Green, *c.*1870. Park Avenue (originally Burgoyne Road) now crosses this site.

82. Willesden House was one of the grander mansions just off the High Road. In 1881 it was the home of Rev. Cleaver seen here with members of his family in the garden.

83. *The Spotted Dog* on Willesden Green was described in 1792 as 'being a well accostomed Publick House', and became one of the favourite places of resort for mid-Victorian Londoners who drove out to 'the country'. This scene, complete with a real spotted dog, dates from about 1860. Note the dove or pigeon boxes on the wall and the entrance to the pleasure ground on the right.

84. *The Old Spotted Dog* at Neasden, seen here *c.*1860, was often in friendly contention with its near namesake. At one time, Twyford brothers were landlords of each. The pub fascia is advertising 'Porter' and 'Entire', strong beers. Bate and Walter's cart delivered groceries and wine from their shop at St George's Terrace on the Hampstead side of Kilburn High Road. This inn has now been renamed *The Old Grange Tavern*.

85. 'Harlesden Park', *c.*1870. As Harlesden expanded, developers submitted imaginative plans for new estates in the surrounding green field areas. Pictured is that for Harlesdon (*sic*) Park, based on the site of the existing 'Hurworth' (see plate 77). All the other buildings are imaginary, including the church and the battlemented house on the left.

86.   A late Victorian photograph of the long-established *Coach and Horses*. It stood by the Stone Bridge over the Brent and was a well-known anglers' inn. Like *The Plough* at Kensal, it was a haunt of the painter George Morland and its position on the main road to Harrow ensured much passing trade.

87.   Furness Brickworks, *c.*1890, another link with George Furness. After his success as public works contractor, he turned to building houses in Willesden, his adopted town. For this he established a brickworks in Chambers Lane. All but one of the people pictured (the man holding the brick mould) are members of the Prettey family. The works were producing a quarter of a million red kiln-burnt bricks every three weeks.

88. Haymaking at Welford's Farm, Harlesden Road, *c.*1900, the haystacks displaying the fine thatching typical of Middlesex farms. At that time Brent was largely given over to the production of hay for London horses. The buildings on the extreme right can also be seen in plate 68.

89. Taken from the architect's drawing of 1870, this is the elegant Kilburn Brewery, originally established in 1822 as the medallion on the entablature indicates. It was rebuilt in the mid-Victorian period whilst run by the brewers Michell and Aldous. It stood just south of Dyne Road and operated until shortly after the end of the Great War.

90. Houses in Llanover Road which were part of a small North Wembley development which also included Peel Road. Plaques on the wall of a building in East Lane (now demolished) bore the initials 'C.A.E.' and the date 1896. Some houses (not illustrated) have party walls projecting through the roofs; visible protection against fire.

91. In preparation for the long-planned but still-delayed Wembley Plaza scheme at Montrose Crescent, many houses were demolished. No. 2 Station Grove, built c.1890, was temporarily converted before its demolition and the sign of a previous owner, F. J. Midson undertakers, was uncovered and is now recorded for posterity. Later it was taken over by another funeral director, S. E. Smith and Son.

92.   Wembley House, 1880. This is another grand mansion which succumbed to the pressures of development. Another of the Page family homes previously stood on this site, but this building, with its tower, was Victorian. John Turton Wooley was one owner, but it was Col. George Topham who developed the estate, which now includes Cecil Avenue and London Road. During the Great War the house became a private school and after demolition the site was used for Copland School (1952).

93.   This is Wembley Park Mansion, also called the White House, c.1880. Built in the 18th century, it was acquired by one of the extensive local Page family, Richard, who engaged Humphry Repton, the famous landscape gardener who worked on Brondesbury Manor and Kenwood House, Highgate, to lay out the grounds. Later it was acquired by the Gray family who made further alterations to the house. All that is left is the thatched lodge at the corner of Wembley Park Drive and Wembley Hill Road and the name of the road – Manor Drive.

94. This is an idealised illustration, *c.*1840, of St Mary's, the first purpose-built school in Willesden, near Willesden church which can be glimpsed through the trees on the left. It first opened as a Sunday School in 1820 and this building was erected in 1840 but demolished in 1976 when a new school was provided a short distance away. The infants' school building still exists in Pound Lane. Next to the signpost a round-house or lock-up can be seen.

95. Acton Lane School was built in 1891/2 and is now Harlesden Primary School. It was the first to be provided by the Willesden School Board under pressure from Whitehall and supplemented the existing church schools. It was the forerunner of many others built to meet the growth in the area's population.

PARISH OF
WILLESDEN.

A VESTRY will be held in the Vestry Hall at Church End, in this Parish, on THURSDAY NEXT, the 1st October, at 6 o'clock in the evening precisely,

To lay before the Vestry a Letter received by the Parish Officers from the Hendon Rural Sanitary Authorities, relative to the Sanitary Arrangements of the Parish after the 29th September, and until the Election of a Local Board.

96. The vestry, the 'council' of the parish, met regularly for hundreds of years, and the records of Harrow and Willesden vestries make interesting reading. This notice convening such a meeting for 1 October 1874 is typical.

97. All Souls' church, Harlesden. As Willesden developed, St Mary's parish was divided and daughter churches built. After Christ Church in Brondesbury came several in Kilburn, including J. L. Pearson's masterpiece, St Augustine's. All Souls' was built in 1879 to E. J. Tarver's design as an octagon, but the nave was removed in 1978.

98. West Kilburn Baptist church. Non-conformist churches were prominent in Brent's religious tapestry. This solid, well-proportioned building dating from 1866 now stands in a more open setting due to the redevelopment of South Kilburn from 1949 onwards.

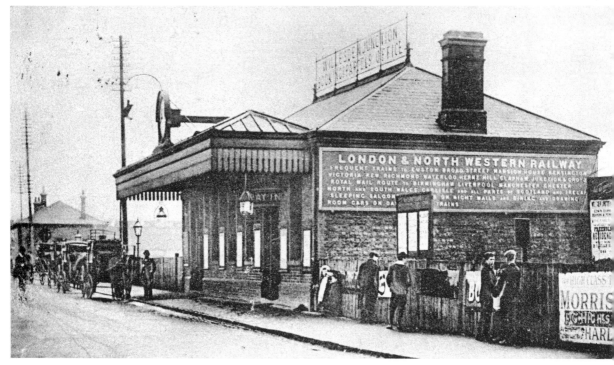

99. Willesden Junction station, *c*.1900. In its heyday, this junction was one of the busiest in Britain, and it was said to be haunted by the ghosts of travellers lost in its labyrinthine passageways. It served the main Euston to Scotland trunk route and local lines to Broad Street, Richmond, Olympia and Watford.

100. Congregational chapel, Chapel End, 1890: the corner of Pound Lane and Willesden Green High Road as seen by E. Batchelor. The chapel still remains virtually unchanged, but the pound (hence Pound Lane, previously called Petticoat-Stile Lane) has been pulled down and replaced by a garage. On the extreme left can be seen St Mary's Infants' School.

101.   Chapel End, also called Queenstown, was named after the chapel in the centre of this picture (*c*.1890) which stood for about 100 years at the corner of Dudden Hill Lane and Willesden Green High Road. This chapel was the predecessor of the congregational chapel in the previous plate and was later used as a Sunday School before being demolished in 1908 for road widening.

102. Fire station at Queenstown, *c*.1890. This picture was taken a few years later than plate 101, the building on the right having a greater covering of ivy. It was used by the Willesden volunteer fire brigade. Samuel (S. E.) Cayford's smithy had several homes before and after this one at Chapel End.

103. 'Watkin's Folly', Wembley Park, 1902. Sir Edward Watkin, a railway builder of renown, conceived Wembley Park as a great London amusement centre. He wanted an eye-catcher to rival the Eiffel Tower; one of his dreams was a Manchester-London-Paris railway through a channel tunnel. Designs were invited and building started, but money ran out and this was its final appearance. In 1907 it was demolished and Wembley Stadium was constructed on the site in 1923.

104. The Metropolitan Railway Works, Neasden, 1923. To service the extension of this railway through Willesden and Wembley to Harrow, a large engineering works was built in 1881/2, the workers being housed at Neasden Village (see plate 105). When the line was electrified a generating station was added. Three, and later four, 3,500-kw turbo-generators were provided and artesian wells sunk to provide water for the system.

105. The provision of the engineering works at Neasden led the well-intentioned Sir Edward Watkin (then Chairman of the Board) to build houses for the workers in 1882. The estate, later called Neasden Village, had streets named after more distant country stations such as Quainton Street (seen here) and Verney Street. In the 1920s the estate was expanded with houses of a special concrete structure by Hamish Cross, which can be seen in the background.

106. Jackman's smithy, Neasden, *c.*1920, well remembered in the district. The family's connection with the area dates from at least 1810. The smithy actually stood beneath the proverbial spreading chestnut tree. By 1926 it was reported that 'they are still there, but their glory and romance are departed'. Today they have vanished completely and Woolworths has covered the site.

107. Kingsbury urban district offices, 1930. A rather prosaic name for an attractive house in Buck Lane at Kingsbury Green. Built c.1910, it was used by the local council (Kingsbury had its own urban district council when it separated from Wembley until it was amalgamated again in 1934) and was also known as the White House. The crossroads are the junction with Church Lane, and the site is now partly covered by Mead Court.

108. In the 1890s Willesden Local Board seized the opportunity to become one of the new district councils and planned a worthy town hall as a civic centre. This is the site c.1885, previously Waterloo Farm.

109. In full top-hatted Victorian splendour, members of Willesden Local Board pose for the ceremony of laying the foundation stone of the town hall in Dyne Road in 1891.

110.   Willesden town hall, *c.*1948. This resplendent Victorian building, completed in 1894, was not considered grand enough to be preserved once Brent came into existence. For 70 years it served Willesden but became redundant when Wembley town hall was chosen as the civic centre of the new borough. This building was replaced with a block of municipal flats named in honour of James Stewart, the first chairman of the district council.

111.   Wembley urban district council offices, 1937. With the formation of the new district council in 1895, the need for a meeting chamber and offices became urgent. Land was acquired the following year at the corner of the High Road and St John's Road. The offices, which stretched down to Ecclestone Mews where there was a fire station and works depot, were sold to British Home Stores in 1962.

112. No. 5 Willesden Green High Road, 1893.
Today this building is a branch of Barclay's
Bank but is virtually unchanged, unlike those on
either side.

113. Elms Lane, a typical country lane which,
in the early 1900s, was still representative of
much of Wembley, Kingsbury, Cricklewood
and Neasden. The two nearest flank-wall
windows of the house on the right have since
been blocked. One of the elms which gave the
road its name can be seen.

114. Wembley Park, *c*.1900. The grounds of the White House (see plate 93) were acquired by Sir Edward Watkin, the railway magnate. He retained the name 'Wembley Park' for the amusement grounds he built, which included a boating lake and golf course and the ill-fated tower (see plate 103). With its own station on the Metropolitan Railway, it proved a popular attraction, as shown by the crowds in this picture.

115. Forty Farm, Wembley, *c.*1910. This long-established farm at Forty Green was known as Pargraves for many years before taking the local name of Forty Farm and, later, South Forty Farm. It was long in the possession of the Page family of Wembley. In the 1920s, as farming declined, it became the headquarters of the Century sports ground.

116. This picture of 1959 shows Hillside as a thriving shopping centre as it was when it was built in the 1890s. Now, except for the two public houses (the *Stonebridge Park Hotel* and the *Orange Tree*), all has changed to make way for the redevelopments of the 1980s. The small but homely houses have been replaced by soulless tower blocks.

117. An early photograph of about 1900 of Harrowdene House at the corner of Napier Road and Wembley High Road.
It was built by Dr. C. E. Goddard, Wembley's first Medical Officer of Health and is now an old people's home called
Charles Goddard House.

118. This is the Maria Grey training college as it looked when it moved to Salusbury Road in 1885. It later became
Brondesbury and Kilburn Girls' Grammar School, and Kilburn Grammar School was built off to the left of the picture.
The outbuilding on the right no longer stands.

119.   Kilburn Grammar School, which opened in 1898, moved to Salusbury Road in 1900. As a boys' grammar school it contributed much to the community in the way of mayors and council staff. It was often regarded as a twin with the girls' school (see plate 118), later became a comprehensive but was closed in 1989.

120.   Dollis Hill House, 1916. This early 19th-century mansion was owned for a time by Lord Aberdeen who frequently invited William Gladstone, the Liberal leader, to stay and rest from his parliamentary exertions. The house and grounds were acquired by the council and laid out as Gladstone Park. The photograph was taken during the Great War when the building was in use as a hospital.

121. Wembley slowly began to succumb to the builders before the Great War, but the council managed to save part of Read's Farm, near Park Lane School, as Edward VII Park. This picture shows the park after the opening ceremony in June 1914 when it was named by G. T. Barham in honour of the recently deceased king.

122. Care of the poor and sick was, until the introduction of the welfare state, undertaken by the community. The Poor Law (abolished in 1948) was administered by Boards of Guardians who were, in Willesden, responsible for building a workhouse infirmary which was opened in 1903 in Acton Lane, opposite Lower Place farm. Most of these buildings still exist as part of Central Middlesex Hospital but the spot where the photographer is standing has become part of a factory.

123. This somewhat formal photograph of Willesden's first public library at Willesden Green shows the building as it was when opened in 1894. It was rebuilt in the 1980s but, after a fierce debate in the council, the charming turreted front section was retained. It was designed by Newman and Newman who were also responsible for Willesden town hall and the cottage hospital.

124. This is Harlesden High Street in 1912 with the 25-year-old jubilee clock prominent. This scene has changed very little.

125. Wembley High Road, 1910, showing the junction with Lancelot Road before Killip's shop was built. Tramlines and wires are visible and many of the buildings are recognisable today.

126. The other end of Wembley High Road in the same year, showing the junction with St John's Road. The Dutch-style gables on the left are repeated on buildings to the right, out of the picture.

127.   Wembley post office, *c*.1900. At this time it was common practice to build short terraces of shops with flats above. Totnes Terrace has virtually disappeared under successive redevelopments, Menzies covering the post office site, although a few of the upper floors remain or have been reinstated in 1890s' style.

128.   These attractive Dutch-style gables at Sudbury Mall are dated 1909, although the buildings on either side are earlier. *The Swan*, further north on Sudbury Green, has been an inn for hundreds of years under various names.

129. The exotic mansion of Lewgars in Kingsbury, seen here *c.*1910, was the result of extensions made to an older building by the antiquarian E. N. Haxell. He used materials discarded in the refurbishment of St Andrew's church in the 1870s. Another sad loss, Lewgars was pulled down in 1952 to accommodate the post-war expansion of Kingsbury.

130. Sutherland House, Kingsbury, *c.*1930. The Duchess of Sutherland had this lovely Tudor-style mansion built in 1899. It had its share of fame when, in 1929-30, John Logie Baird used it in his early television trials. It became a home for the elderly and also houses the Kingsbury Veterans' Club.

131.   A steam navvy on the Wembley cutting of the Great Central Railway during construction in 1902. 'Watkin's Folly' (see plate 103) can be seen in the background with Neasden Hill behind it. The house on the left is in Wembley Hill Road.

132.   Wembley Hill station on the Great Central Railway in 1915, later known as Wembley Stadium station. The low building on the right was the booking office. The shops, with flats above, are dated 1908.

133. This was the cottage-style Willesden Green station in 1910, with plenty of advertisements and city-bound gentlemen.

134.   This early electric locomotive is at Neasden, en route to Harrow, *c.*1910. It was the pride and joy of the Metropolitan Railway in the first phase of electrification before the Great War.

135.   The tram terminus, Willesden Green, seen in 1907 from the Conservative Association office. The scene is hardly recognisable today, since virtually all the buildings, as well as the tramlines, have gone.

136. Vernon House, Willesden Lane. One of a number of grand villas in this lane, Vernon House like its neighbours was built in the first flush of the 'discovery' of Brondesbury Heights as a pleasant out-of-town home for the middle class of Victorian London. Access to the city was via the nearby North London line. This villa later became the Willesden Education Office and then a special school in Brent, but may soon be demolished. Christ Church, built in 1866, can be seen in the background of this picture.

137. Roe Green village, *c.*1920. During the Great War, Kingsbury became a sizeable aircraft and munitions production centre, with a small aerodrome off Stag Lane. To help house workers from the factories, the government commissioned the building of an estate at Roe Green. The village shown here with one of the factories in the distance was barely under construction when the war ended. The charm of the estate is maintained under a conservation order.

138. Lloyd George promised 'Homes for Heroes' after the Great War, and Housing Acts were the prosaic response. From 1920 onwards, these houses were built at Stonebridge on the St Raphael estate alongside what was to become the North Circular Road.

139. Kingsbury fought a losing battle with Whitehall, claiming it could not afford to provide municipal housing. These houses in Highmeadow Crescent, built in 1922, were the attractive rebuttal of their protestations.

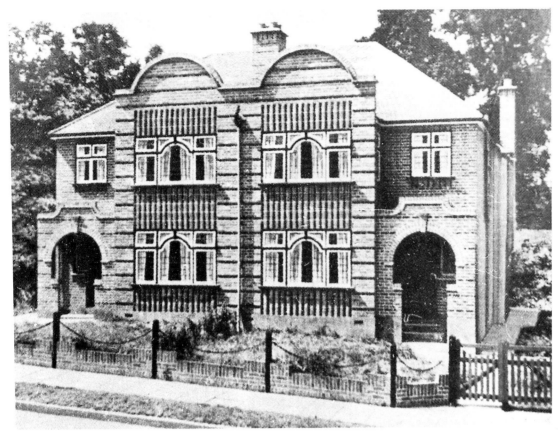

140. The inter-war development of Wembley, mainly by private builders, made it one of the fastest-growing districts in London. F. and C. Costin developed much of Kenton, including the Woodcock Dell estate. Here on the Lyon Farm estate are Nos. 11 and 13 Regal Way, a pair of the more interesting houses, built around 1935. Unfortunately, one of the pair has now had its leaded windows replaced by the ubiquitous panoramic double-glazed type and others have been stone-clad.

141. Comben and Wakeling were building partners who started in St John's Road before the Great War and became one of the three or four major developers of suburban Wembley. Their show-houses at the junction of Wembley Hill Road and Wembley Park Drive reveal Tudor-style timber-framed façades. Three of the five corners at this junction boast pairs of houses like these at Nos. 2 and 4 Wembley Park Drive, built around 1932.

142. In the Edwardian period, much of the Mapesbury estate was built with well-designed houses like this one of 1908, White Hall, at the corner of Dartmouth and Mapesbury Roads. The estate is now a conservation area.

143. At No. 238 East Lane, on the Sudbury Court estate, stands one of the loveliest houses in Brent. 'Villa D'Este' was built in 1932 by Eric Wakeling (son of one of the founders of the building firm) for his own use, enhancing the already attractive Sudbury Court estate.

144. The building of suburban Wembley, 4 May 1936. This photograph shows the south-western slope of Barn Hill, with The Avenue running across the picture and Mayfields the road on the right. The new branch line to Stanmore curves across from the left to the extreme right.

145. E. G. Trobridge was one of Britain's most original architects and operated, for the most part, in the Kingsbury area. He revived thatched roofs for urban houses in the 1930s as this and other houses in Buck Lane show. The interiors are equally and excitingly different. His houses can also be found in Colin Deep Lane, Hendon (Nos. 89 to 105).

146. Trobridge Flats, Buck Lane. Trobridge also built a 'folly' at each of the four corners of the junction of Buck Lane with Wakeman's Hill Avenue and Highfield Avenue. They are much more comfortable than their exteriors would suggest.

147. This is the approach to Wembley Park station in 1923 just before the crowds came thronging to the British Empire Exhibition. There was an additional entrance on the eastern (right-hand) side of the bridge next to Barclay's Bank. The area where the station name stands is still empty, but the other three corners of the crossroads are now covered by offices.

148. Queensbury station under construction, 1932. Kingsbury was the last area of Brent to be developed, but once building started the rate was phenomenal. The name for this area, Queensbury, was chosen in a newspaper competition to match Kingsbury. Such development encouraged London Transport to extend the Bakerloo Line from Wembley Park through Kingsbury and Queensbury to Stanmore. Thus this site was prepared, while a biplane flew from Stag Lane aerodrome.

149. & 150. This pair of photographs show opposite sides of Albert Road before and after the slum clearance which began in 1948. The same two cars are visible in each, as one side of the road was still to be improved by Willesden Council. The houses in this road were built in the 1870s.

151. An early factory to come to Kingsbury was Desoutter's who made artificial limbs. One of the Desoutter family had been a pilot who flew from Kingsbury and who lost a limb in an accident. Their works were in rural Kingsbury, seen here in 1923 with Hay Lane to the top left. The open-top bus in Edgware Road is advertising Haig whisky.

152. This empty site at Park Royal was taken on by Guinness who hired Sir Giles Scott, who had built Liverpool Cathedral and Waterloo Bridge, to build a factory in 1934. It became Guinness' main brewery in England.

153. The Guinness factory under construction, 1933. This brick building was typical of the period which also produced Battersea power station.

154. This photograph shows something of the size of the Post Office Research Station on Dollis Hill. It is a landmark for miles around even though the radio aerials have now gone. It opened in 1934 and continued until the early 1970s when it became a commercial estate, partly occupied by Willesden College of Technology. During the war, its deep basements were occasionally used for cabinet meetings by Winston Churchill.

155. Willesden cottage hospital was built in 1894 with a benefaction from J. Passmore Edwards. This watercolour was painted in 1922, and the scene is little changed today.

Mr. G. H. Ward | Mr. J. W. Comben | Mr. W. J. Coaley | Mr. H. F. Frankl | Mr. A. T. Coucher | Mr. A. Hewitt

WEMBLEY HOSPITAL—FRONT ELEVATION

Mr. J. A. Phelp | Dr. R. H. Martin | Dr. T. O'Callaghan | Mr. W. C. Cowell | Mr. E. Butler, J.P. | Mr. J. W. Gordon, J.P.

156. Opened in 1926, Wembley hospital was one of the many products of G. T. Barham's philanthropy. Although much enlarged, the original building has not changed significantly since the day Barham opened it.

157. Dollis Hill synagogue was built in 1938 by Sir Owen Williams, of British Empire Exhibition and Empire Pool fame, using a similar ferro-concrete style. Some windows are in the traditional Shield of David (Magen David) shape. Many of the older synagogues in Willesden have now closed as the Jewish community they served has now moved further out to Wembley and beyond to Harrow, Pinner and Northwood.

158. Sudbury Town station, *c.*1950. With the nationalisation of London Transport in the early 1930s, Frank Pick, its general manager, was able to carry through a complete restyling of lettering, logo and buildings. The architect, Charles Holden, designed clean-lined, attractive and distinctive stations like Sudbury Town and Alperton on the Piccadilly Line.

159. This building, seen here *c.*1870, was originally Willesden High School, a name much later appropriated for one of Brent's comprehensive secondary schools. It became a film studio for a few years in the 1920s and is now the county court at Craven Park.

160.   Willesden Hippodrome a year or so after it opened, *c*.1910. It was part of the circuit for all the great stars in the heyday of music hall, including G. H. Elliott (who lived in Willesden and in Oakington Avenue, Wembley) and Marie Lloyd. In 1927 it was bought by the young Sidney Bernstein, later of Granada fame. It was destroyed by a bomb in 1940 and was eventually replaced by government offices.

161.   After the invention of cinematograph film, public showings of the new artistic form of entertainment developed rapidly. Initially, local halls were hired for the purpose, but soon a series of 'dream palaces' were opened. There were several in Willesden including the lavish Rutland Park cinema in Willesden Green High Road shown here in 1912, now sadly demolished.

162. Gaumont State cinema, Kilburn. When building was started, this was to be the world's largest cinema; by the time it was opened, by Gracie Fields and other stars in 1937, it was Europe's largest, with 4,004 seats. It was the pinnacle of the cinema world's success as a public entertainment, but within 20 years was hit, like all other cinemas, by the advent of television. Now most of the building is given over to bingo, with a very small cinema hidden inside. However, the magnificent foyer is still maintained, chandeliers and all. It is, at present, the only cinema operating in the whole of Brent.

163. As the suburbs of London expanded in the 1930s, new shopping centres sprang up at Kingsbury, Kenton and here at Neasden. This view of the Shopping Parade was taken in 1947, with the roundabout junction of the North Circular Road and Neasden Lane visible in the background. In the 1970s, the lane was diverted into an underpass, leaving the shopping centre as a cul-de-sac.

164. & 165. Willesden's Borough Day, 1933. To achieve borough status was the ambition of many district councils in London. Willesden was granted its Charter in 1933, Wembley in 1937. All Willesden schoolchildren were presented with a commemoration certificate.

LABORARE EST ORARE

Willesden

Presented to

Sylvia Shackman

a scholar at *Furness Rd Girls'* School

to commemorate the grant by

His Majesty King George V.

of a Charter of Incorporation to the inhabitants of Willesden.

The presentation was made at King Edward VII.

Recreation Ground and the Charter was delivered to

the Charter Mayor (COUNCILLOR GEORGE H. HISCOCKS) by

the Right Hon. the Lord Mayor of London

(SIR PERCY GREENAWAY)

on Thursday, the 7th day of September 1933.

Town Hall,
Dyne Road,
   N.W.6.

Chairman of the Council.

166. Freddie Hall invented stamp-vending machines and the telephone coin-box. His factory was in Dudden Hill Lane and workers are seen here making the boxes in about 1950. The firm later underwent a series of takeovers until, in 1982, it ceased to operate, partly as a result of the introduction of new style telephone kiosks and equipment.

167. In the 1970s, a new style of glass-clad building began to appear. Tretol House at the corner of Holmstall Avenue and Edgware Road in Kingsbury is one of the early examples.

168. Station House, Stonebridge, was the first of the tall office blocks to come to Brent in 1965 although, fortunately, there have not been many. This building dominates the junction of the Harrow Road and North Circular Road near Stonebridge Park station. It is seen here after the 'topping out' ceremony conducted by the first mayor of Brent, councillor John Hockey.

169. Another contemporary architectural style is demonstrated by this all-glass building at Wembley Park. Originally occupied by Levi Strauss, it is now used by B.A.S.F.

170. Wembley (now Brent) town hall, *c*.1950. The town hall built by Clifford Strange for the new Wembley Council, impressing Pevsner the architectural historian, was barely ready when war broke out in 1939. With the formation of the new borough in 1964, it became Brent's town hall. It is a modern, clean-lined building, but not large enough for all its staff.

171. & 172. In July 1879 one of the series of Royal Agricultural Shows was held in Queen's Park, Willesden. One hundred acres of land north of the Birmingham Railway were devoted to a display of modern farming equipment, animals and foodstuffs (*above*). It was opened by the Prince of Wales (later Edward VII), and Queen Victoria, who herself exhibited farm animals, visited later in the week. All was well planned apart from the weather (*below*) – 'Exhibition' and 'mud' became synonymous in London at that time.

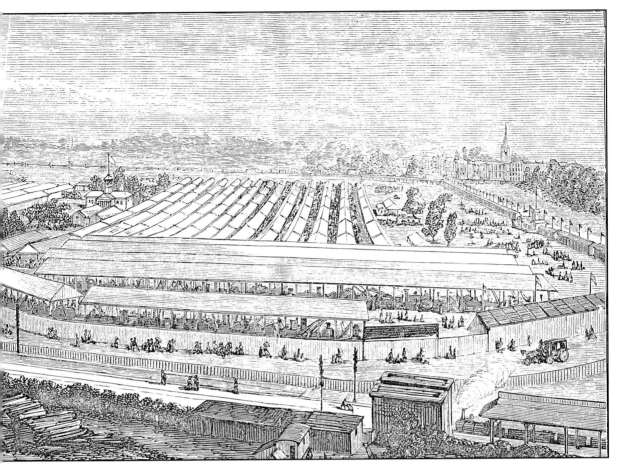

173.   This picture of the British Empire Exhibition under construction in 1923 shows some of the largest 'palaces' and gives an impression of its overall size. Some of the 'new' houses on the Chalk Hill (Metroland) estate are in the background.

174.   The British Empire Exhibition of 1924 and 1925 was the biggest event to take place in Brent. This is the Malaya Building, complete with minaret.

175.   The Palace of Arts was one of a number of buildings using ferro-concrete on a large scale for the first time. It is one of the few buildings remaining from the Exhibition, although in need of repair.

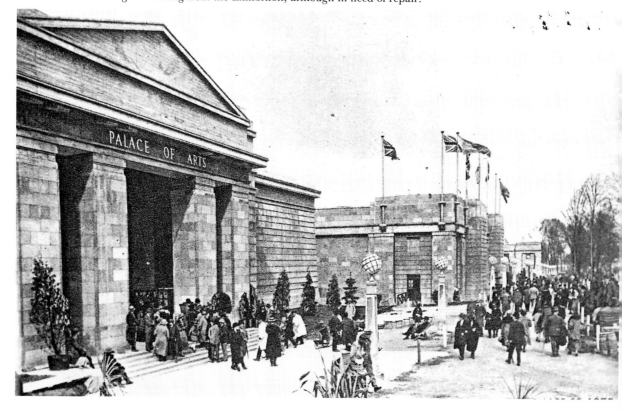

176.   One of the most prominent features of the British Empire Exhibition was the sports stadium which has given Wembley a world-wide reputation ever since. During the first match, the Football Association cup final of 1923 between Bolton Wanderers and West Ham United (2-0), it was full to overflowing. This is the scene in 1950 with the Oakington estate being built on the far right.

177.   Ten years after the Exhibition the same engineer, Sir Owen Williams, came back to build the Empire Pool. At the time it had the largest concrete-spanned roof in the world. The water was heated, with artificial waves, and there was a tropical garden. It closed during the war and was never again used for swimming, except during the Olympic Games. It is now the Wembley Arena, used for ice-skating, shows and pop concerts.

178.   Wembley Stadium extended its use to many other sports, including greyhound and motor-cycle racing. In 1948, the Olympic Games were again held in Britain and Wembley was the centre. Here, straining every muscle, are the marathon runners.